160201

HAPP

a melodr ngs

lyrics by
BERTOLT BRECHT
music by
KURT WEILL
original German play by
DOROTHY LANE
book and lyrics adapted by
MICHAEL FEINGOLD

SAMUEL FRENCH, INC.
25 West 45th Street   NEW YORK 10036
7623 Sunset Boulevard HOLLYWOOD 90046
LONDON   TORONTO

Amateurs wishing to arrange for the production of HAPPY
END must make application to SAMUEL FRENCH, INC., at
25 West 45th Street, New York, N.Y. 10036, giving the following particulars:

(1) The name of the town and theatre or hall in which
    it is proposed to give the production.
(2) The maximum seating capacity of the theatre or hall.
(3) Scale of ticket prices.
(4) The number of performances it is intended to give,
    and the dates thereof.
(5) The title, number of performances, gross receipts &
    amount of royalty & rental paid on your last musical
    performed.

Upon receipt of these particulars SAMUEL FRENCH, INC.,
will quote the terms upon which permission for performances
will be granted.

Stock royalty quoted on application to Samuel French, Inc.,
25 West 45th Street, New York, N.Y. 10036.

For all other rights than those stipulated above apply to
Bertha Case, 345 West 58th Street, New York, N.Y. 10019.

**For music royalty terms and material apply directly to
European-American Music Corporation, 11 West End
Rd., Totowa, N.J. 07512. Telephone: (201) 256-7100.**

**Anyone presenting the play shall not commit or autho-
rize any act or omission by which the copyright of the
play or the right to copyright same may be impaired.**

**No changes shall be made in the play for the purpose
of your production unless authorized in writing.**

Printed in U.S.A.

ISBN 0 573 68190 2

A TRUE STORY WITH A "HAPPY END"

by Michael Feingold

In 1928, the young writer-composer team of Bertolt Brecht and Kurt Weill had reached the height of its prewar fame. The success of *The Threepenny Opera* had converted Brecht, the outspoken avant-garde poet, and Weill, the intensely serious atonal musician, into Brecht-&-Weill, the clever musical comedy duo whose smash hit (within a year of its opening, *Threepenny Opera* had received over thirty European productions) had the whole continent whistling its seductive pop tunes and quoting its cynical couplets.

This kind of middlebrow popular success actually sat rather awkwardly on the two men, and the fallout from *Threepenny* left both of them preoccupied with more serious projects. Brecht, who had recently embraced Marx's economic theories, was working on his giant capitalist tragedy, *St. Joan of the Stockyards*, while Weill had returned to his most ambitious theatre project to date, the full-length opera *Rise and Fall of the City of Mahagonny*, the composition of which had been interrupted by the hasty execution of *Threepenny* shortly after Brecht finished drafting the libretto (expanded from the 1926 *Mahagonny Songplay* or "Little" *Mahagonny*, their first collaboration). For the moment, they thought, they were through with the commercial theatre.

That they were not is due to the persistence of one man, the ebullient producer Ernest Josef Aufricht, who was not about to let the sources of his huge *Threepenny* success get away so easily. Aufricht proposed that, for the fall of 1929, Brecht and Weill write him a contemporary sequel to *Threepenny Opera* (which had been based on John Gay's 18th century *Beggar's Opera*, updated by Brecht to Queen Victoria's time), to be produced with the same cast, at the same theatre in Berlin (the cosy Schiffbauerdam, now the home of the Berliner Ensemble), opening on the first anniversary of *Threepenny's* memorable opening night.

3

The promise of redoubled fame and fortune made Aufricht's offer hard to resist, and Brecht quickly started casting about for a suitable story to adapt. Elisabeth Hauptmann, his faithful secretary, had the answer, discovered in the course of her exhaustive English-language reading (she was the one who had translated *The Beggar's Opera*, after its triumphant London revival by Nigel Playfair, and proposed it to Brecht in the first place). To this day no one is certain exactly what Hauptmann's English source was; to avoid copyright problems the story was credited to a mythical "Dorothy Lane" and described as having appeared in the nonexistent "J. & L.. Weekly, St. Louis." The similarity to the plot of *Guys and Dolls* has led many to speculate that Damon Runyon was the source of *Happy End*. Unfortunately for them, Runyon's story "The Idyll of Miss Sarah Brown," from which Frank Loesser's musical is drawn, didn't appear in print till the early 1930s.

A romance between a Salvation Army worker and a street tough, however, was no surprise in the fictional conventions of the time. Bernard Shaw, one of Brecht's early idols, had opened up the stage possibilities of the material in *Major Barbara* (1905), in which the aristacratic Barbara has an intense confrontation with a surly dockside laborer, Bill Walker (note the similarity to the name Bill Cracker). And *Major Barbara*, reset in Chicago with details lifted from Upton Sinclair's *The Jungle*, was Brecht's starting point for *St. Joan of the Stockyards*. Another likely source was Edward Sheldon's *Salvation Nell* (1909), an early triumph of the American realist movement led by the popular actress Minnie Maddern Fiske, who made a huge success in the central role of a goodhearted slum girl, saved by Army preaching, who struggles to rescue her common-law husband from gin and fisticuffs. One of Nell's cohorts is a popular hellfire preacher nicknamed Hallelujah Maggie, and the first act is set in a saloon on Christmas Eve.

Brecht and Hauptmann, in any case, embroidered freely on whatever they took from their unidentified source or sources, inventing with their politics, their complexly European vision of America, and the specific abilities of their actors in mind. A sinister Oriental modeled on the silent film roles of Sessue Hayakawa was an obvious role for Peter Lorre, who had worked well with Brecht at Munich in *The Jungle of Cities;* a gangster who robbed banks in women's clothes, improbably, was an amusing one for the portly Kurt Gerron, who had made a hit as Tiger Brown. Carola Neher, who had given up the lead role of Polly Peachum in *Threepenny* at the last moment to be at her dying husband's bedside, would play the heroic Salvation Army lass, while the gang would be filled out with two Brechtian favorites, Oscar Homolka (who had played *Baal* and Mortimer in *Edward II*) and Theo Lingen (who had given a memorable performance as the Clown in the *Badener Lehrstueck* the year before).

Actors whose old-fashioned attitudes had caused clashes with Brecht in *Threepenny* rehearsals were quietly passed over: The slick operetta tenor Harald Paulsen (Macheath, who latter rejoined the team for *Mahagonny*), the cabaret *diseuse* Rosa Valletti (who had refused to sing Mrs. Peachum's "filthy" song about sexual slavery), the stodgy Erich Ponto (Peachum) were not to be seen in *Happy End*. Most notable of the omissions was Kurt Weill's wife, Lotte Lenya, whose performance as Jenny had made her the toast of Berlin. Her absence, however, was not due to Brecht but to the enterprise of Moritz Seeler, director of the prestigious Berliner Volksbühne's *Junge Bühne*, or second stage, which had signed her for an adventurous season that included *Danton's Death* (Lenya played Lucile Desmoulins) and the still scandalous *Spring's Awakening* (Lorre, joining the company after *Happy End* closed, played a memorable Moritz Stiefel to her Ilse).

Brecht's wife, however, was definitely present. Helene Weigel, whom he had recently married and who shared both his new Communist beliefs and his esthetic militancy, was cast as the Lady in Gray- She had regarded *Threepenny Opera* (in which she played the small role of the brothel madam) as a severely compromised work from a political point of view, and was determined to see that no such compromise afflicted *Happy End*. It hardly needs to be said that this was not what Aufricht and his crew had in mind. The script had turned out to be a jolly escapist romp with a few leftist gibes along the way, its acid undercurrent getting lost in the "collaborative" bedlam that accompanied any Brecht rehearsal, and Weigel apparently grew more and more dissatisfied.

Accounts of what actually took place on opening night of *Happy End* (September 2, 1929 — exactly a year and two days after the opening of *Threepenny*) differ markedly. We know that the first two acts passed without incident, and were favorably

received. Lenya remembered Weill telephoning her backstage
at intermission, to say he was sure they had a hit. The third
act, however, was marred by a fatal incident: The Lady in
Gray's final speech, which seems harmless enough in the text
as it stands, aroused violent booing and whistling (the tradi-
tional European expression of displeasure) from the expensive
seats, which in turn stimulated shouts and counter-arguments
from the gallery, precipitating a near-riot. Some assert that
Brecht had rewritten Weigel's speech privately with intent to
provoke, others that she improvised a diatribe against capitalism, still others that she pulled a notorious Communist Party
broadside from the pocket of her costume and began to ha-
rangue the audience with excerpts from it.

Whatever the source of the provocation, the middle-class part
of the audience was duly provoked, and to make matters worse,
Brecht and director Erich Engel had contrived to follow the
speech with an ironic hymn to capitalism (now traditionally
used as the Prologue) which called for the emergence onstage
of mock stained-glass windows representing Saint Rockefeller,
Saint Henry Ford, and Saint J. P. Morgan. To a German bourgeois audience with a sizeable respect for both religion and
money, this was the last straw, and the first-nighters responded
with yells, threats, and what one reviewer described as a "con-
cert of whistling." The critics, barely escaping with their
dignity intact, gave Brecht and company a thorough belaboring
in the next day's papers, with B.B.'s arch-enemy, the staid and
influential Alfred Kerr, mocking the work's derivations with
the phrase *"Happy entlehnt"* ("happily borrowed" — it was
Kerr who had accused Brecht of plagiarizing Villon in the
Threepenny lyrics), and suggesting that Engel would do better
to write plays himself than to get them from such as Brecht.
The other critics followed Kerr's lead, with even Brecht's loyal
supporter Herbert Jhering complaining that the last tableau
appeared to belong to an entirely different play. (He was not
far from wrong: Its lyric, along with several other key sections
of *Happy End*, turned up the next year in *St. Joan of the
Stockyards*.) The ticket-buying public, dismayed by the notices
and fearful of riots, shunned the work, which closed two days
later, an ignominious failure.

Brecht subsequently repudiated the script, crediting it in his
notes on *St. Joan* entirely to Hauptmann. When it was finally
revived in 1958, she followed suit, instructing the German

publisher to use only the name "Dorothy Lane" on the title
page. (At the request of her heirs, her name was reinstated
following her death in 1977.) They were right to do so; the
original version, despite some amusing moments, is a desperately casual makeshift, which just happens to serve as a dramatic
setting for some of the greatest theatre songs ever written.
The present version is a free adaptation, which treats the
"Dorothy Lane" script as loosely as the collaborators of 1929
treated their mysterious source. Only the lyrics, whose author-
ship Brecht never denied, have been kept in more or less literal
translation.

If *Happy End* was a setback for Brecht, for Weill it was a pure
victory. The songs, as interpreted by Lenya and countless
other artists, are among the keystones of his reputation, and
have kept the idea of the show alive even when its script seemed
totally unfeasible. Over the years, the score has served as
a sort of reservoir from which people could draw music for
other Kurt Weill shows: "The Bilbao Song," in New York,
was interpolated into the Off-Broadway *Threepenny Opera,*
Anglicized by Marc Blitzstein as "Our Bide-a-Wee in Soho."
The lyric of the "Mandalay Song" was given a new setting by
Weill for the "Loving" scene of *Mahagonny,* and several of
the Salvation Army hymns turned up in Weill's Paris musical
Marie Galante, four years later, as decidedly profane French
dance-hall tunes, with "In Our Childhood's Bright Endeavor"
becoming "The Young Girls of Bordeaux." Since the current
adaptation was commissioned by Robert Brustein's Yale Repertory Theatre in 1972, numerous American productions have
been given, with a Broadway production (featuring former
Yale Rep actors Meryl Streep and Christopher Lloyd) spear-
heading the Kurt Weill revival that has lately engulfed New
York. *Happy End* in its latest incarnation has found its way
to Australia and Wales, to British and American resident
theatres, universities, and to London's West End. Despite its
stormy beginnings, *Happy End* is now thriving, to use a word
Brecht coined for the occasion, *happyendlich.*

HAPPY END was first performed in the U.S. by the Yale Repertory Theatre, New Haven, on April 6, 1972. It was directed by Michael Posnick, with the following cast:

THE PROFESSOR............................. *Ralph Drischell*

THE REVEREND............................... *David Hurst*

BABY FACE................................. *James Brick*

SAM "MAMMY" WURLITZER.................... *Jeremy Geidt*

DR. NAKAMURA............................. *Alvin Epstein*

MIRIAM................................. *Rosemary Stewart*

BILL CRACKER............................. *Stephen Joyce*

THE COP................................. *Paul Schierhorn*

THE FLY................................. *Elizabeth Parrish*

SISTER LILLIAN HOLIDAY............... *Stephanie Cotsirilos*

SISTER MARY................................. *Joan Welles*

SISTER JANE............................. *Sarah Albertson*

BROTHER HANNIBAL JACKSON.............. *John McAndrew*

BROTHER BEN............................. *Herb Downer*

MAJOR STONE............................. *Nancy Wickwire*

TWO MEN................................. *William Peters*
Yannis Simonides

8

It was subsequently produced on Broadway by Michael Harvey and the Chelsea Theatre Center, at the Martin Beck Theatre, on May 7, 1977, with the following cast:

THE PROFESSOR.............................. Robert Weil

THE REVEREND.............................. John A. Coe

BABY FACE..............................Raymond J. Barry

MAMMY.............................. Benjamin Rayson

DR. NAKAMURA.............................. Tony Azito

MIRIAM.............................. Donna Emmanuel

BILL CRACKER......................... Christopher Lloyd
(later replaced by Bob Gunton)

THE COP................................. David Pursley

THE FLY................................. Grayson Hall

SISTER LILLIAN HOLIDAY..................... Meryl Streep
(later replaced by Janie Sell)

SISTER MARY.................... Prudence Wright Holmes

SISTER JANE........................... Alexandra Borrie

BROTHER HANNIBAL JACKSON.................. Joe Grifasi

BROTHER BEN......................... Christopher Cara

MAJOR STONE.............................. Liz Sheridan

9

CHARACTERS

THE GANG:

BILL CRACKER
SAM "MAMMY" WURLITZER
DR. NAKAMURA ("THE GOVERNOR")
JIMMY DEXTER ("THE REVEREND")
BOB MARKER ("THE PROFESSOR")
JOHNNY FLINT ("BABY FACE")
A LADY IN GRAY ("THE FLY")
MIRIAM, the barmaid

THE SALVATION ARMY:

MAJOR STONE, female
CAPTAIN HANNIBAL JACKSON
LIEUTENANT LILLIAN HOLIDAY
  ("HALLELUJAH LIL")
SISTER MARY
SISTER JANE
BROTHER BEN OWENS

ALSO:

A COP
MEMBERS OF THE FOLD

PLACE: Chicago

TIME: December 1919

ACT ONE: Bill's Beer Hall. December 22.

ACT TWO: The Salvation Army Mission, Canal Street.
      December 23. (Inset: The Beer Hall)

ACT THREE, SCENE 1: The Beer Hall. December 24.

ACT THREE, SCENE 2: The Mission. Later than night.

10

MUSICAL NUMBERS

PROLOGUE.......................... ENTIRE COMPANY

ACT ONE

"THE BILBAO SONG" .... GOVERNOR, BABY FACE, BILL,
and THE GANG
"LIEUTENANTS OF THE LORD" .. LILLIAN and THE ARMY
"MARCH AHEAD" .... THE ARMY
"THE SAILORS' TANGO" .... LILLIAN

ACT TWO

"THE SAILORS' TANGO" (Reprise) .... LILLIAN
"BROTHER, GIVE YOURSELF
A SHOVE" .... THE ARMY and THE FOLD
"SONG OF THE BIG SHOT" .... THE GOVERNOR
"DON'T BE AFRAID" ..... JANE, THE ARMY and THE FOLD
"IN OUR CHILDHOOD'S BRIGHT ENDEAVOR". HANNIBAL
"THE LIQUOR DEALER'S
DREAM" .... HANNIBAL, GOVERNOR, JANE, ARMY, and FOLD

ACT THREE, SCENE 1

"THE MANDALAY SONG" .... SAM and THE GANG
"SURABAYA JOHNNY" .... LILLIAN
"SONG OF THE BIG SHOT" (Reprise) .... BILL
"BALLAD OF THE LILY OF HELL" .... THE FLY

ACT THREE, SCENE 2

"THE HAPPY END" .... FINALE—THE ENTIRE COMPANY
SONG OF THE BIG SHOT — Reprise
IN OUR CHILDHOOD — Reprise
LIEUTENANTS OF THE LORD — Reprise
THE BILBAO SONG — Reprise

PROLOGUE

Limbo. The ENTIRE COMPANY *huddled together in a tight group. Only faces visible. Slides: The portraits of presidents on dollars bills blown up huge and tinted like the pictures of saints on stained glass windows. Alternative: Giant stained-glass caricatures of St. Henry Ford, St. John D. Rockefeller, and St. J. P. Morgan.*

COMPANY (*Sings*)
PRAISE TO THE FORDS AND ROCKEFELLERS —
    HOSANNAH!
THE BUYERS AND THE SELLERS — HOSANNAH!
ALL POWER TO THE GREAT — HOSANNAH!
GIVE THEM THE CITY AND THE STATE —HOSANNAH!
HOSANNAH! HOSANNAH! HOSANNAH! HOSANNAH!

(*Blackout. Music changes to a raucous foxtrot. The slides, moving in tempo with the music, change to a series of stills of the cast in costume, with the character's name and the actor's name superimposed on them, in the style of old movie credits. The series opens with "The management of this theatre proudly presents HAPPY END, by Bertolt Brecht and Kurt Weill," and, when the entire cast has been shown, changes to authentic period photographs of Chicago, emphasizing the poor, the Salvation Army, wealthy people on Michigan Avenue, crowded slums, etc. Over the last of these, just as the Prologue music ends, is projected the title: CHICAGO/DECEMBER 1919. In the second of silence between the Prologue and Act One, a new title is flashed on the screen by itself: BILL'S BEER HALL — A WAY STATION ON THE ROAD TO HELL.)*

HAPPY END

ACT ONE

Bill's Beer Hall. Late afternoon. Winter. A bar with a row of stools. Pianola to one side. Prominent on the other wall, a hatrack with many hats on it. Exit to back room behind bar. A view of the street outside, possibly a flight of steps leading to it.

It is late afternoon outside, but the barroom is dimly lit. MIRIAM *is at the bar, washing glasses, tough, disinterested.* THE PROFESSOR *is seated in a chair downstage center, wearing a hat, coat, and scarf.* HE *has a false moustache on and affects a thick German accent.* HE *is writhing in the glare of a high-intensity lantern held by* THE REVEREND. BABY FACE *stands menacingly over him, wearing brass knuckles.* SAM *looks on anxiously nearby, and* DR. NAKAMURA *watches from upstage, hidden in the semidarkness.*

PROFESSOR. (*Getting up, as if trying to escape*) Pliss—
BABY FACE. (*Pushing him back down*) Siddown, kraut!
PROFESSOR. But mine vife und children —
BABY FACE. Siddown, I said, or I'll ram dese brass knuckles down yer troat!
SAM. Now hold on there, Baby Face. We can treat the gentleman better than that, can't we?
BABY FACE. Well, he ain't been treatin' us so good, and I'm fed up. He's gonna get his face bashed in.
SAM. (*Jumping in between* BABY FACE *and* PROFESSOR) No, don't hurt him! He didn't mean to do us dirt. He's a nice guy. Aren't you, Mr. Prinzmeyer?
PROFESSOR. Pliss — I haff a vife and children — pliss —
SAM. You see, he's a nice guy, He'll play along. The Governor's gonna give him another chance, wait and see. What do you say, Governor?
PROFESSOR. Pliss —

13

NAKAMURA. (*From the darkness*) He have been warn three time already.

BABY FACE. Lemme at him!

SAM. No, Baby Face! Governor, I appeal to you. Give the fellow a break. He's a good man. Why, he's even a Elk.

NAKAMURA. (*Coming forward*) Step out of way, Sammy. Mr. Pharmacist Prinzmeyer, I will explain once again: Do you wish your drugstore be protected from criminals?

PROFESSOR. Ja — ja.

NAKAMURA. If you want protection, you must to pay us every month. Otherwise, who know what may transpire?

PROFESSOR. But I haff told you, I haff no money. Mein vife is ein zick voman. Pliss —

NAKAMURA. Do not trifle with us, Mr. Pharmacist. Is unwise. Have you ever heard of — The Fly?

PROFESSOR. Vot — vot iss der Fly?

NAKAMURA. If you miss payment, Mr. Prinzmeyer, will come a day when mysterious woman in gray stop you on street and ask for light for her cigarette. That is signal, Mr. Prinzmeyer. From that moment, you are marked man. When you light cigarette for The Fly, flame of your life soon snuffed out.

PROFESSOR. (*Weeping*) Nein, nein.

NAKAMURA. Reverend! Please to show our friend hat collection!

(*The lantern that has been aimed at* PROFESSOR'S *face swivels to the hatrack, wobbles*)

NAKAMURA. A little higher, Reverend.

REVEREND. Sorry, Governor. This contraption's awfully hot.

(*The* PROFESSOR *squirms in his chair, starting to say something*)

BABY FACE. Siddown, you!

NAKAMURA. Do you see hats on wall, Mr. Prinzmeyer? They have been collected by our friend Bill Cracker. Do you know him?

(*Lantern wobbles again*)

NAKAMURA. Higher, Reverend.

REVEREND. Extremely sorry.

NAKAMURA. When he hang hat so high in air, head that once

wore hat six feet underground. Care to see your hat on rack, Mr. Prinzmeyer?

PROFESSOR. Nein — nein.

NAKAMURA. Then think again, please. Will you pay to us, or no? Let us read answer on Mr. Prinzmeyer's face, Reverend.

(*Light does not move*)

NAKAMURA. Light, Reverend.

(*Light does not move*)

NAKAMURA. Reverend!

REVEREND. I'm sorry. I can't hold that infernal thing a minute longer!

PROFESSOR. (*Ripping off false mustache*) Dummy, why don't you grip it the way I showed you?

(*As* PROFESSOR *gets up and starts arguing with* REVEREND *about the lantern,* BABY FACE *tries to make him sit back down and* SAM *tries to make* ALL *of them go back into the scene. Three counts of ad libbed bedlam*)

NAKAMURA. (*Topping the bedlam*) Stop! (*Silence*) Light, Miriam.

(MIRIAM *switches on the bar lights.* EVERYONE *relaxes — we see that it's only a rehearsal*)

NAKAMURA. We do it one more time, gentlemen. And this time we get it right.

PROFESSOR. Can we take a break first? That light's killin my eyes.

REVEREND. If you'd put a handle on that damn reflector —

PROFESSOR. If you'd just hold it the way I showed ya —

REVEREND. I have better things to worry about than your metallic imbecilities.

(PROFESSOR *starts to answer back,* NAKAMURA *interrupts him*)

NAKAMURA. (*Sharply*) We have all to worry about this. Prinzmeyer is president of Mercantile Association. If he refuse to pay us protection, they will all refuse. We cannot countenance rebellion.

SAM. I got a new idea. If you can work out a way to send them out of the room and let me talk to him alone —

NAKAMURA. Is too complicated —

SAM. — then I can work in my organ as a compromise offer.

NAKAMURA. Organ??

SAM. That church organ we picked up in the St. Luke's job last month. I ain't found a way of unloading it yet. I'll get old Prinzmeyer to buy it on time — that's how we'll get the payments out of him —

NAKAMZRA. (*Cutting* SAM *off, somewhere around "on time"*) Sam!

(SAM *quickly shuts up*)

NAKAMURA. Please to keep your organ out of shakedown operation. This serious business. (HE *sees* MIRIAM *going to* PROFESSOR *with a cloth for his eyes, takes it away from her and throws it at* PROFESSOR) Beer, Miriam.

(MIRIAM *silently draws a beer and brings it to* NAKAMURA. *As* HE *takes it from her,* REVEREND *pinches her fanny.* SHE *turns to him angrily, but decides not to say anything and goes back behind the bar.* MEN *laugh*)

PROFESSOR. (*Throwing cloth back at* MIRIAM) Oh boy, Jimmy. You wouldn't do that if Bill was here.

BABY FACE. Where is Bill, anyways?

PROFESSOR. Yeah, we need him for this job, ya know.

REVEREND. That's right. Our threats won't mean diddly-squat if we can't back them up.

PROFESSOR. So when is Bill gettin' back?

BABY FACE. (*Overlapping*) Yeah, what's takin' him so long?

REVEREND. (*Overlapping at the same time*) Yes, he'd better be here soon.

NAKAMURA. (*Cutting them off*) Gentlemen, please! Mr. Cracker will be back today. If not, he will be replace tomorrow. In any case work will proceed. Fly has ordered.

(*Thud of a newspaper hitting the front door. All duck,* NAKAMURA *motions to* BABY FACE, *who cautiously goes to the door*)

BARY FACE. Hey, da paper's here.

(ALL *relax*. HE *brings paper in*)

BABY FACE. I got dibs on the funnies. (*Unfolding paper, glances at headline*) Hey, look at this: "BAXLEY GANG ROBS TRAIN."

(EVERYONE *reacts*. BABY FACE *reads*)

BABY FACE. "Niagara Falls, New York — special dispatch. Concerned citizens looked on in horror yesterday evening as the infamous 'Gorilla' Baxley gang robbed the Chicago-Buffalo express train of over twenty thousand dollars in cash and gold bull-lion."

(*By this time* ALL *are on their feet and moving towards* BABY FACE. *On* "*twenty thousand dollars*" THEY ALL *stop dead, in unison*)

SAM. Twenty thousand dollars!
PROFESSOR. Wait till Bill hears about this!
BABY FACE & REVEREND. (REVEREND *is now looking over* BABY'*s shoulder*) Sh! This gang of bullies further outraged respectability continued on page fourteen."
BABY FACE. Huh?
REVEREND. Well, turn it, lunkhead!

(BABY FACE *turns page*. ALL *are now clustered around paper*)

BABY FACE & OTHERS. "by boarding the train at Niagara Falls depot disguised as a wedding party. This mockery of the Christian sacrament was compounded by the repulsive Baxley himself being costumed as the bride. It is time, surely, for a new reign of law and order."
SAM. Twenty thousand dollars!
BABY FACE. Bill's gonna explode!
PROFESSOR. He hates Baxley's guts anyway.
REVEREND. Baxley, Baxley, Baxley. Why don't *we* get breaks like that?
GOVERNOR. Calm, gentlemen. Our turn yet to come.
REVEREND. Sure, like Christmas.
NAKAMURA. Do not mock, Reverend. Important news arrive soon.
SAM. That's right, the Fly said we had a big job coming up.

REVEREND. Well, we know her idea of a big job — shaking down some kraut druggist for six bits and a bottle of Sloan's Liniment. I ask you, what kind of professional crime is that?

GOVERNOR. (*Firmly*) Promote calm on troubled water, Reverend.

REVEREND. Calm? This gang is so calm it's got rigor mortis. You'd think it was impossible for a crook to earn a decent living. But it's not: Look at Gorilla Baxley. I have to admire a man like that, even if he is our competition. He has enterprise; he aims high. And as my sainted mother used to say, a man who aims high is a great man. Not some penny-pushing gunslinger like our Bill. Gorilla Baxley is a great man. Gorilla Baxley is ambitious, Gorilla Baxley is imaginative, Gorilla Baxley is —

BILL. (*Who has come in unobserved during this.* HE *is holding a battered homburg, His face is bruised.*) Dead.

EVERYONE. BILL!!

(*Title on screen:* BILL CRACKER—HIS TOUGH EXTE- RIOR CONCEALED A HEART OF STONE. BILL *goes to the hat rack and hangs the homburg with the other hats.* HE *takes a piece of chalk from his pocket, and chalks above the hat the initials G. B.*)

BILL. That's time for you, Reverend. Yesterday a great man — today a little inkblot in the Book of Life.

(GANG *crowds over to shake* BILL'S *hand and ad lib congratulations.* MIRIAM *throws him the keys to the bar*)

BILL. Thanks, sweetheart.

NAKAMURA. A fine achievement, Bill. Congratulations. (*Pulls him downstage, away from the* OTHERS) Fly isn't going to like this at all.

BILL. Stick the Fly. I can handle her. I can handle the both of youse. (HE *breaks away from* NAKAMURA *and goes up to bar*)

NAKAMURA. (*To* EVERYONE) My friends, appropriate to celebrate. With Gorilla out of way, Chicago ours to run. Bill's Beer Hall will be center of underworld.

BABY FACE. Awright!

NAKAMURA. It will be greatest place since original Bill's Beer Hall in Bilbao.

BABY FACE. I never heard of it.

NAKAMURA. Have you got a nickel?

BABY FACE. Sure.

NAKAMURA. Then I tell you all about it. (*Puts nickel into pianola, which lights up*) I don't remember all words, but Bill can help out.

BILL. Thanks, but no thanks. (*Sits at bar, turning his back to* NAKAMURA. *Title: "THE BILBAO SONG"*)

NAKAMURA. (*Sings*)
BILL'S BEER HALL IN BILBAO, BILBAO, BILBAO
WAS THE MOST FANTASTIC PLACE I'VE
    EVER KNOWN.
FOR JUST A DOLLAR YOU'D GET ALL YOU WANTED,
    ALL YOU WANTED, ALL YOU WANTED
OF WHATEVER KIND OF JOY YOU CALLED YOUR OWN.
BUT IF YOU HAD BEEN AROUND TO JOIN THE FUN
WELL, I DON'T KNOW IF YOU'D HAVE LIKED
    WHAT YOU'D HAVE SEEN.
THE STOOLS AT THE BAR WERE DAMP WITH RYE.
ON THE DANCE FLOOR THE GRASS GREW HIGH.
THROUGH THE ROOF THE MOON WAS SHINING
    GREEN.
AND THE MUSIC REALLY GAVE YOU SOME
    RETURN ON WHAT YOU PAID.
(HEY, JOE, PLAY THAT OLD SONG THEY
    ALWAYS PLAYED!)
        THAT OLD BILBAO MOON
        DOWN WHERE WE USED TO GO

— Who remembers the words?

        THAT OLD BILBAO MOON

— It's just too long ago!

I DON'T KNOW IF
IT WOULD HAVE BROUGHT YOU JOY OR GRIEF
BUT
IT WAS FANTASTIC
IT WAS FANTASTIC

IT WAS FANTASTIC
BEYOND BELIEF

BABY FACE.
BILL'S BEER HALL IN BILBAO, BILBAO, BILBAO
CAME A DAY THE END OF MAY IN NINETEEN-EIGHT
FOUR GUYS FROM FRISCO CAME WITH BAGS OF
    GOLD DUST, BAGS OF GOLD DUST, BAGS OF
    GOLD DUST
AND THE TIME THEY SHOWED US ALL
    WAS REALLY GREAT!

BUT IF YOU HAD BEEN AROUND TO SEE THE
    FUN, WELL,
I DON'T KNOW IF YOU'D HAVE LIKED
    WHAT YOU'D HAVE SEEN:
THE BRANDY BOTTLES SMASHING EVERYWHERE
AND THE CHAIRS FLYING THROUGH THE AIR
— THROUGH THE ROOF THE MOON STILL
    SHINING GREEN
'N THOSE FOUR GUYS ALL GOING GRAZY,
    WITH THEIR PISTOLS BLAZING HIGH.
THINK YOU CAN STOP 'EM? WELL, GO RIGHT
    AHEAD AND TRY!
        THAT OLD BILBAO MOON

— Can't remember the words

        THAT OLD BILBAO MOON

— Something with "Love" in it

I DON'T KNOW IF
IT WOULD HAVE BROUGHT YOU JOY OR GRIEF
BUT
IT WAS FANTASTIC
IT WAS FANTASTIC
IT WAS FANTASTIC
BEYOND BELIEF!

    BILL. (*Turning around*) Awright, I got a good one for yez!
(*Sings*)
BILL'S BEER HALL IN BILBAO, BILBAO, BILBAO
NOW THEY'VE CLEANED IT UP AND MADE IT
    MIDDLE-CLASS

WITH POTTED PALMS AND ICE CREAM,
  VERY BOURGEOIS, VERY BOURGEOIS
JUST ANOTHER PLACE TO PUT YOUR ASS!

BUT IF YOU SHOULD COME AROUND TO SEE THE FUN
WELL, I DON'T KNOW, YOU MIGHT NOT FIND IT
  SUCH A PAIN
    (Huh!)

THEY'VE MOPPED UP ALL THE BOOZE AND
  BROKEN GLASS.
ON PARQUET FLOORS YOU CAN'T GROW GRASS.
THEY SHUT THE GREEN MOON OUT BECAUSE
  OF RAIN.
AND THE MUSIC MAKES YOU CRINGE NOW,
  WHEN YOU THINK OF WHAT YOU PAID.
(HEY, JOE, PLAY THAT OLD SONG THEY
  ALWAYS PLAYED!)

(BILL *shouts the lyrics between phrases, and the* OTHERS *pick
    them up and sing them. It's obvious that* HE'S *the only
    one who knows the song*)

  EVERYBODY.
THAT OLD BILBAO MOON
DOWN WHERE WE USED TO GO
THAT OLD BILBAO MOON
CASTING ITS GOLDEN GLOW
THAT OLD BILBAO MOON
LOVE NEVER LAID ME LOW
THAT OLD BILBAO MOON
WHY DOES IT HAUNT ME SO?

I DON'T KNOW IF
IT WOULD HAVE BROUGHT YOU JOY OR GRIEF
BUT
IT WAS FANTASTIC
IT WAS FANTASTIC
IT WAS FANTASTIC
BEYOND BELIEF!
  BILL. (*Spoken*) And it's all over now!

(*The sentimental lighting that has come up on them for
    the song suddenly fades. Lights up very bright on the*

street. A LADY IN GRAY *enters.* THE COP *catches her and carries her into the saloon. Title on screen: A MYSTERI-OUS GUEST!! Projection: A housefly)*

COP. Hey, fellas, this old dame passed out in the street all of a sudden!

(Ad libs of concern. MIRIAM *brings a glass of water and hands it to* COP. SAM *and* PROFESSOR *help* LADY *into chair.* ALL *gather round)*

REVEREND. *(Not looking at her)* Why, she's barely breathing!
COP. She might have broken her ankle or something. I'll get a cab to take her to the hospital.
PROFESSOR. Better move fast, it's rush hour.

(Exit COP. *Dead silence for a second. Then* BILL *takes a step towards* LADY IN GRAY)

BILL. Fly?
LADY. *(Coming to life)* God, what an ugly puss. What happened to you?
BILL. I tripped on a lump of dirt—Gorilla Baxley.
FLY. Gone?
BILL. *(Indicating hat)* G-O-N.
FLY. Very interesting.

*(*THE GANG *has gathered around her, putting their weapons on the table.* SHE *goes up to* BABY FACE *and pulls from his jacket a gun* HE *has kept concealed)*

FLY. How you doing, Baby Face?
BABY FACE. Aw, not bad.
FLY. Good boy. Things running smoothly, Governor?
GOVERNOR. Pretty well, thank you, boss.
FLY. All right, men. Item One: The bank job you've all been waiting for is scheduled for the day after tomorrow.
ALL. Christmas Eve!!
FLY. Ho ho ho.
GOVERNOR. Brilliant!
REVEREND. Which bank?
FLY. You'll find out. Item Two: Last week's car heist. Well, Bill? You were gone a long time. We were getting worried.

BILL. Thanks for your concern. I got the cars to Detroit, fresh coat of paint, unloaded them real easy. We cleared eight hundred bucks, it's waiting for you in the usual place. With receipts for my expenses.

FLY. Very good. Did you happen to run into Tessie Miller in Detroit?

(MIRIAM *breaks a glass.* GANG *snickers*)

BILL. What if I did?

FLY. Well, it doesn't really matter. It's just that I saw Tessie today. She had a new silver fox piece around her neck, Bill. She said it was a gift from a friend, Bill. She told me it cost three hundred dollars, Bill.

BILL. Three hundred clams, my, my.

FLY. Three hundred clams. My, my.

BILL. Don't you wish you had friends like that?

FLY. (*Taking out a cigarette*) Could you give me a light, Bill?

(BILL *lights her cigarette.* GANG *stares in horror. As match strikes, title on screen: THE FATAL FLAME! Freeze onstage breaks when* FLY *exhales*)

FLY. Governor, you remember the matter we discussed earlier?

GOVERNOR. (*Purring*) Certainly.

FLY. We'll go ahead with that plan. Item Three: You've rehearsed the Prinzmeyer Pharmacy job, right?

GOVERNOR. All set to go, boss.

FLY. Good. That seventy-five bucks a month means a lot to us.

BILL. More chicken feed.

FLY. You can sit this one out, Bill. For the rest of you, the Pharmacy's at the corner of Jackson and Fifteenth. Sam and Baby, the back door. Professor, lookout.

PROFESSOR. But I —

FLY. Don't interrupt! Governor, you and the Reverend take the front door. We're going to make a nice example of Mr. Prinzmeyer. All right, you can have your rods back. It's time for the Fly to buzz off.

SAM. Wait a minute, there's something else! Where am I going to unload that goddam church organ? I'm out three hundred fifty —

COP. (*Offstage, getting closer*) "That old Bilbao moon, la la la la ... "

FLY. (*Sotto voce*) You'll have to work that one out for yourself.

COP. I'm back. I finally got a cab.

(FLY *faints in his arms*)

COP. She all right?

GOVERNOR. (*Mock-puzzled*) Oh, she just seem to be coming round.

COP. Well, I better get her to a hospital. (HE *carries* THE FLY *out. The* OTHERS *hold till* THEY *exit. ALL are uncomfortable in* BILL's *presence. Title on screen: A TICKLISH SITUATION!*)

BABY FACE. Bill, I just wanna say ...

(GOVERNOR *stops him. Pause. Dead silence*)

BILL. Awright, lay off! What the hell is this, an old ladies' home?

BABY FACE. Bill, you don't understand.

BILL. (*Roughing him up*) Don't tell me I don't understand, jocko. You think I don't know what's going on around here? You think I gotta read it in Braille? I ain't afraid to light no broad's cigarette, no matter what it means. And I can take you guys on one at a time or altogether. So if any of you gimps wants to see your chapeaus up there on a nail behind Dr. Wakasaki — you can meet me in the back room! (*Exit* BILL, *glowering*)

REVEREND. Well, we all know what we have to do. But how, may I ask, are we going to do it?

BABY FACE. I dunno.

REVEREND. Of course not.

BABY FACE. Lay off!

PROFESSOR. There's gotta be a way out of this, lemme think ...

SAM. (*Sarcastic*) Maybe you'll think of some gadget that when he touches it, he bumps hisself off.

PROFESSOR. Say, you know, that's not a bad idea, lemme see ...

GOVERNOR. (*Quietly and authoritatively*) Gentlemen. (THEY ALL *look up*)

GOVERNOR. Not to worry. Mr. Cracker will be put out of way without any help from us.

(*Ad lib confusion from* GANG)

GOVERNOR. You recall minor job to be done this evening on unfortunate pharmacist?

(*Ad libs: "Yeah, so what about it?"*)

GOVERNOR. When we perform such job, is usually no evidence. This evening, will be evidence. Gentlemen, I give you — and the police — (HE *display's* BILL's *gun, which* HE *has palmed or pick-pocketed during* FLY's *exit, wrapped in his silk handkerchief*) Mr. Cracker's revolver.

(*Gasps of astonishment from* GANG)

REVEREND. A veritable genius!
BABY FACE. Hey, that ain't fair!
GOVERNOR. (*Smiling*) Very perceptive, Baby Face. (HE *pokes* MIRIAM, *who has buried her face in her hands, with his cane*) Beer, Miriam.

(*Tableau. Lights dim on saloon and come up on street, where the* SALVATION ARMY — MARY, JANE, HANNIBAL, *and* BEN — *marches on, led by* LILLIAN HOLIDAY. *Title on screen:* MEANWHILE, VIRTUE MOBILIZES)

LILLIAN. (*Sings*)
LOOK ALL AROUND YOU
LOOK ALL AROUND YOU
LOOK ALL AROUND YOU, A MAN IS ABOUT TO DROWN
A WOMAN IS SCREAMING "HELP ME,"
    A CHILD IS FALLING DOWN.
DON'T MOVE ANOTHER STEP!
STOP, STAY RIGHT THERE!
PEOPLE NEED HELP ALL AROUND YOU —
DON'T YOU EVEN CARE?
ARE YOU COMPLETELY BLIND?
YOU'VE TIME TO GREET YOUR BROTHER,
    BUT NONE FOR ALL MANKIND!
FORGET ABOUT YOUR DINNER
HAVE YOU FORGOTTEN, SINNER

HOW MANY STAND IN LINE?
HOW MANY STAND IN LINE?
I KNOW YOU'LL SAY, "THE POOR ARE ALWAYS
  WITH US."
"THE WORLD'S UNJUST AND THAT'S
  HOW IT WILL STAY."
HERE'S HOW WE ANSWER YOU:
  YOU'VE GOT TO STAND UP
FORGET YOUR FEARS AND FIGHT WITH US TODAY.
SO BRING ON THE TANKS AND THE CANNON
AND SQUADRONS OF PLANES LET THERE BE
AND BATTLESHIPS ON THE SEA
JUST TO CONQUER ONE SMALL BOWL OF SOUP
  FOR EVERY POOR MAN
JUST TO CONQUER ONE SMALL BOWL OF SOUP
FOR EVERY POOR MAN!

LILLIAN & ARMY. (*Sing*)
LET EVERY MAN COME JOIN US
OUR MISSION TO FULFILL
THE ARMY THAT IS SMALL BUT STRONG
IS MADE UP OF MEN OF GOOD WILL

LILLIAN.
FORWARD MARCH, CHIN UP, TAKE WEAPONS,
  PREPARE
PEOPLE NEED HELP ALL AROUND YOU —
  SO YOU'VE GOT TO CARE!

(*Lights come up immediately on bar, as* ARMY *marches in*)

LILLIAN. God's blessing on all here!
PROFESSOR. Sweet Jesus!
LILLIAN. (*Distributing tracts*) It is never too late to think
of Jesus, brothers.
BABY FACE. (*Grabbing her*) Do ya love your neighbor,
sister?
LILLIAN. Stop that, brother. A man can't love his fellow
humans until he loves the Lord. We will sing to stir your souls.
Number five, "March Ahead." Brother Hannibal.

(HANNIBAL *blows pitch pipe*)

ARMY. (*Sings*)
MARCH AHEAD TO THE FIGHT
WHERE SATAN'S POW'R IS AT ITS HEIGHT
SING YE NOW, USE YOUR MIGHT
LET YOUR SONG RING THROUGH THE NIGHT
SOON YOU WILL SEE THE MORNING LIGHT
AND WITH THE MORNING OUR LORD JESUS CHRIST
HALLELUJAH!

PROFESSOR. Ya know, it's kind of catchy.

REVEREND. (*Very exaggerated*) Oh, sister, you have moved me. I should like to repent.

SISTER MARY. A convert already!

LILLIAN. Sing with us, brother!

(THEY *repeat the hymn,* REVEREND *joining in*)

PROFESSOR. About time we saw you praying, Reverend.
(GANG *laughs*)

LILLIAN. Shame on you! This man wants to forsake his life of sin, and you just laugh!

REVEREND. Pay no attention to them, sister. Your singing does my heart good. I am a miserable sinner, but I feel comfort in the presence of a holy person such as yourself. (HE *is on his knees next to her, embracing her, etc*)

LILLIAN. (*Disentangling herself*) Brother . . .

BABY FACE. Oh, brother!

REVEREND. I feel I can confide in you, Sister — Sister — what is your name, Sister?

SAM. And what's your telephone number?

(GANG *laughs*)

LILLIAN. I am Sister Lillian Holiday.

REVEREND. (*Passionately*) Sister Lillian!

LILLIAN. (*Trying to escape him*) And this is Sister Mary, and Sister Jane, Brother Ben Owens, and Brother Hannibal Jackson with the trombone.

PROFESSOR. (*Aside to* GOVERNOR) She's the one they call "Hallelujah Lil" — the Saint of South Canal Street!

GOVERNOR. Most edifying.

BABY FACE. She's got some build on her for a saint!

(GANG *laughs.* LILLIAN *starts to rebuke them*)

REVEREND. Don't mind them, Sister Lillian. Let me tell you my story. I was brought up without benefit of your divine guidance. My Ma, rest her soul, kept me alive by selling her body. And when she died, my dad sold it again, to the medical students. All for my sake!

MARY. Ugh!

REVEREND. It's true, Sister. And as a consequence, it was inevitable that my hands should of strayed onto other people's property for a rather large proportion of my life.

JANE. Not so, brother.

REVEREND. Not when the blessed Army is here to rescue me, Sister. For I deeply resent the error of my ways, now that I feel closer to you — and to God. My remorse is great.

PROFESSOR. Ain't it the truth?

(GANG *laughs*)

REVEREND. But I want to make a clean breast of my sins. I want to donate all my ill-gotten gains to the cause.

(JANE *comes forward with collection basket*)

HANNIBAL. (*Beaming*) We know the saying: There is more joy in Heaven —

REVEREND. (*Droping all piety*) Over *us* than there is over you, for sure — so *here's* my contribution. (*Spits in basket and throws it back at* JANE, *who shrieks*)

LILLIAN. Shame on you, brother! I've had enough! I'm going to preach you a sermon!

PROFESSOR. (*To* REVEREND) Oh, boy! Now look what you got us in for!

LILLIAN. (*During the sermon the* GANG *razzes her, reacts in exaggerated horror, tries to flirt with her, etc., gradually getting more menacing*) The topic for today's sermon, brother, is the rat. Isaiah 66:17, "The abomination and the rat, they shall come to an end together, saith the Lord." Now, I think you all know what a rat is: It's a dirty little animal that lives in the worst part of town.

BABY FACE. Here we is, sweetheart.

LILLIAN. A rat is a troublemaker, brothers. A rat stinks of garbage the way a drunken man stinks of whiskey. A rat carries disease, as a hoodlum carries his gun and blackjack. (*Wandering among them,* SHE *has come to the* GOVERNOR *and picked up his cane to gesture with. Now* SHE *pulls it apart, does a take when* SHE *sees blade inside, nervously hands it back)*

PROFESSOR. Easy there, Sister.

LILLIAN. (*Regaining her energy*) He lives in the darkest, dirtiest holes he can find. He hides from the good people who live in the poor parts of town, the ones who only want to live right and walk decently with their Lord. Because that's not what a rat wants, brothers.

BABY FACE. And what does he want, dollface?

LILLIAN. He wants to live off those good people, creep out of his hole when they're not looking and steal the bread from their mouths. That's why decent people hate rats. And you . . . (*Pause*) are rats.

SAM. (*Quizzically*) Now I never looked at it in that light before.

(At this point BILL *enters unobtrusively from the back room. The* GANG *has not taken* LILLIAN's *insult lightly, though* THEY *restrain their anger. Their behavior starts to get less frivolous and more menacing)*

LILLIAN. But there's a way out for the rat, brothers.

BABY FACE. (*Trying to grab her*) Yeah, what?

LILLIAN. The rat could reform —

REVEREND. Could he now?

LILLIAN. — clean himself up —

PROFESSOR. I'll bet.

LILLIAN. Come out of his hole and — and get a decent job, so to speak.

GOVERNOR. And be a decent church mouse!

LILLIAN. Yes he could, brother, he could! But he doesn't!

SAM. Aw, too bad.

LILLIAN. And do you know why?

BABY FACE. No, why, beautiful?

LILLIAN. Because he's afraid?

(THEY are surrounding her now: SHE *resists panic)*

LILLIAN. Yes, brothers, a rat is a coward. It doesn't take courage to commit his crimes — just a shortage of policemen and a dark street. But he's afraid to come in out of the darkness, because he's got no faith. He thinks the whole world's made of rats like him, because a rat who knifes a good man

in the back on Monday will knife his brother rat on Tuesday.
So don't be a rat! Don't live in fear and darkness: Come into
the light of Jesus and live decent! Because the rats will turn
against you in the end, but Jesus is always with you!

BABY FACE. (*Grabbing her*) I'm with you, baby!

(*The* GANG *closes in on her. The* ARMY *tries to break through*)

LILLIAN. (*Inside the din*) Let go of me.

BILL. (*Over all the hubbub*) GET YOUR MEAT HOOKS
OFF HER!

(EVERYONE *quiets down*)

BABY FACE. Jesus, Bill, I'm sorry.

BILL. You get these Holy Rollers out of here, and fast.

HANNIBAL. (*Hand to forehead*) Come along, sisters. We've
been wasting our time.

MIRIAM. (*Suddenly running from behind bar*) Oh, God,
take me with you! Get me out of this awful place.

(THE ARMY *looks at one another, astonished.* GANG *laughs*)

BILL. Awright, you Benedict Arnold. Now get out of here,
all of youse, before I throw you out.

HANNIBAL. Come, sisters. Oh, my poor head.

LILLIAN. Well, I'm staying.

BILL. Oh, you are, are you?

(THE ARMY, *with* MIRIAM, *has reached the top of the stairs*)

LILLIAN. Brother Hannibal, if I'm not back in two hours,
bring help.

HANNIBAL. (*Exiting*) God go with you, sister — and pre-
serve me from the migraine I'm getting.

(ARMY *exits.* BEN, *the last out, gives one last loud boom on
his bass drum as* HE *goes*)

BILL. So you're staying.

LILLIAN. You may be the notorious Bill Cracker, but you
don't frighten me.

BILL. Oh, don't I?

LILLIAN. King Nebuchadnezzar was a bigger crook than you,

and he didn't frighten Daniel.

BILL. King who?

LILLIAN. King Nebuchadnezzar. He ruled his gang with an iron fist, but even he couldn't stand up to God. And when it was over, they threw him out and he had nothing but grass to eat.

PROFESSOR. Can we get you a plate of grass, Bill?

BILL. Shuddup! Hey, don't you guys have a job to do or something? Beat it while your shoes are good.

GOVERNER. (*Ironic smile*) Only too glad to oblige, Bill.

(*The* GANG *piles out the back door.* BABY FACE, *as* HE *reaches door, starts to tell* BILL *something*)

BABY FACE. Hey, Bill, they want to —

GOVERNOR. Not wise, Baby Face. (BABY FACE *leaves, upset.* GOVERNOR *takes one last look at* BILL) Goodnight, Miss Hallelujah Lillian. Goodbye, Mister William Cracker.

(HE *leaves.* BILL *watches him go, takes a bottle of whiskey from the bar, pours two drinks, brings them over to a table*)

BILL. The bums! You have to sew your pockets shut to keep their hands out. Siddown!

(LILLIAN *sits, nervously*)

BILL. Now tell me about this king what ate the grass. What was his name?

(*The lights begin to fade, slowly*)

LILLIAN. (*Lifting shot glass nervously*) N-Nebuchadnezzar.

BILL. (*Clinking glasses with her*) Likewise.

(*Fadeout. Title on screen: Slide 1—WHEN THE ARMY OF THE LORD DOES BATTLE . . . Slide 2 — CUPID OFTEN CALLS THE SHOTS. When the lights come up again, it is late evening. There are several empty whiskey glasses on the table in front of* LILLIAN)

LILLIAN. You've got it all wrong. You've misjudged us, admit it. You've had the wrong idea of us all these years, just

like that king had of Daniel, the one who ate grass, what was
his name?

BILL. Nebuchadnezzar.

LILLIAN. Right. He repented of his ways, and joined the
Salvation Army — and that's what you should do, too.

BILL. Maybe I should.

LILLIAN. You're wasting your life. You don't need murders
and thefts and hard liquor to keep you happy. The Army is
always happy. It's music and light and joy. That's why I came
to work there, for the joy. I want to see people happy, and so
does the Army.

BILL. You want 'em to be happy your way.

LILLIAN. I keep telling you, you've got us wrong. We're not
afraid to see things your way. (*Impulsively,* SHE *jumps up and
gives him a quick kiss.* THEY *are both a little embarrassed by
this*)

BILL. . . . All that drum beating and those songs about Jesus.

LILLIAN. We have songs that don't have anything to do with
Jesus!

BILL. I can guess what they're like.

LILLIAN. I bet you can't! (*Getting up shakily*) I need a hat
for this. Have you got a sailor hat?

(*Going up to hatrack before* HE *can answer,* SHE *puts on Gorilla Baxley's homburg*)

LILLIAN. Now this is a common song, about the life of common sailors. Listen.

(*Title on screen above: THE SAILORS' TANGO. Light dims
to a very harsh white spot on* LILLIAN. BILL *watches
raptly.* SHE *sings*)

LILLIAN. (*Singing*)
HEY THERE, WE'RE SAILING OFF TO
    BURMA THIS EVENING
WITH ENOUGH GOOD SCOTCH ON BOARD
    TO FLOAT ALL THE WAY
PLUS A CRATE OF GREAT CIGARS: "HENRY CLAY"
HAD IT UP TO HERE WITH GIRLS, SO WE'RE LEAVING
'CAUSE IT'S TIME TO START A BRAND NEW DAY
YES, IT'S TIME TO START A BRAND NEW DAY.

NOW, WE NEVER EVER SMOKE OTHER
    BRANDS OF CIGARS

AND THIS LEAKY TUB WILL BARELY GET US TO
   BURMA
AND WE DON'T NEED THAT GOD
   WHO'S UP THERE IN THE STARS
AND WE DON'T NEED ALL HIS LAWS ON TERRA
   FIRMA
SO ALL RIGHT, GOODBYE!
AND THE SHIP SAILS AWAY, AND IT MAY REACH
   RANGOON
AND AS FOR GOD, WELL, WE DON'T GET HIM
AND IT MAY BE THAT GOD FEELS JUST THE SAME
   ABOUT US
SO LET'S HOPE HE DOESN'T LET IT UPSET HIM
AND ALL RIGHT, GOODBYE!

WE'RE OFF ON THE SEA AND IT'S
   "WHO GIVES A DAMN?"
LIFE'S PERFECT, 'CAUSE NOTHING IS MISSING
AND YOUR DREAMS OF GLORY? JUST TAKE 'EM
   AND SCRAM!
THE WHOLE WORLD'S OUR POT AND — WE'RE
   PISSING!

AH, THE SEA IS BLUE, SO BLUE
AND ALL THE WORLD GOES ON ITS WAY
AND WHEN THE DAY IS OVER
WE START ANOTHER DAY
AH, THE SEA IS BLUE, SO BLUE
AND THAT'S HOW IT'S GONNA STAY
AH, THE SEA IS BLUE, SO BLUE
AH, THE SEA IS BLUE, SO BLUE
AH, THE SEA IS BLUE, SO BLUE
THE SEA IS BLUE.

HEY THERE, WE MIGHT GO TO A MOVIE IF YOU
   WANT TO
THEY'LL MAKE US PAY, WE DON'T CARE, ME AND
   YOU
WE WON'T GROW OUR GRAY HAIRS, NOT UNTIL
   THEY'RE DUE
PEOPLE LIKE US ARE ENTITLED TO HAVE A BIT
   OF FUN, TOO
'CAUSE THERE'S NOT A THING WE HAVE TO DO
NO, THERE'S NOT A THING WE HAVE TO DO.

NOW, WE NEVER SMOKE CIGARS THAT COST LESS
   THAN FIVE CENTS
AND THAT CHEAP BLACK BREAD GIVES US
   INDIGESTION
AND WE DON'T GIVE A DAMN WHAT MAKES OTHER
   GUYS TENSE
AND AS FOR SOUL-SEARCHING — THERE'S JUST
   NO QUESTION:
THAT'S NOT WHY WE'RE HERE!
AND OUR LIFE SAILS AWAY, AND WHO KNOWS HOW
   IT ENDS?
AND AS FOR GOD, WELL, LET'S FORGET HIM
AND IT MAY BE THAT GOD FEELS JUST THE SAME
   ABOUT US
SO LET'S HOPE HE WON'T LET IT UPSET HIM
YEAH, WHY SHOULD HE CARE?

OUR LIVES ARE OUR OWN AND WE DON'T GIVE
   A DAMN
LIFE'S PERFECT, 'CAUSE NOTHING IS MISSING
AND YOUR DREAMS OF GLORY? JUST TAKE 'EM
   AND SCRAM!
THE WHOLE WORLD'S OUR POT AND —WE'RE
   PISSING!

AH, THE SEA IS BLUE, SO BLUE
AND ALL THE WORLD GOES ON ITS WAY
AND WHEN THE DAY IS OVER
WE START ANOTHER DAY
AH, THE SEA IS BLUE, SO BLUE
AND THAT'S HOW IT'S GONNA STAY
AH, THE SEA IS BLUE, SO BLUE
AH, THE SEA IS BLUE, SO BLUE
AH, THE SEA IS BLUE, SO BLUE
THE SEA IS BLUE.

(*Spoken over music*)
Now all we need is for a storm to blow up!
Relax, there's the docks of Rangoon up ahead.
  — Hey, wait, that's only a bank of black clouds in the air!
Jesus . . . and the waves are going crazy out there!
Jesus, in a minute the whole lot of us will be dead!

(*Sings again*)
WELL, WE KNEW WE'D HAVE TO DIE SOMEWHERE
YEAH, WE KNEW WE'D HAVE TO DIE SOMEWHERE

DOWN GOES THE SHIP AND SOON THE SEA WASHES
  OVER
NOTHING BUT SHARKS DOWN THERE TO SHOW A
  DROWNED MAN THE WAY
SCOTCH IS NO USE TO THEM, OR CRATES OF
  "HENRY CLAY"
WHERE THEY'RE GOING THERE ARE NO GIRLS WHO
  NEED A LOVER
THEY WON'T EVER SEE ANOTHER DAY
THEY WON'T EVER SEE ANOTHER DAY

AND THE WATER COMES UP, AND THE SHIP'S GOING
  DOWN
AND AS FOR A HARBOR, WE DON'T GET ONE
JUST A WRECK OF A SHIP AND A GLIMPSE OF A
  SHORE
BUT OF COURSE, ONE CAN'T LET IT UPSET ONE!
SO ALL RIGHT, GOODBYE!
THEN FOR ONCE, YOU DON'T HEAR ALL THAT BIG
  TALK IN THE AIR
AND THE BIG TALKERS SUDDENLY LOOK SMALLER
AND THEY'RE DOWN ON THEIR KNEES AND
  MUMBLING ABOUT THEIR FATHER WHO'S
  UP THERE
AND THEY'RE STARTING TO WEIGH THE SINS THEIR
  SOULS MUST BEAR
AND THAT'S HOW THEY DIE.

AND NOW LET ME TELL YOU A FACT THAT WE ALL
OUGHT TO KNOW:
WHEN YOU STAND BEFORE THE THRONE WHERE
  OUR LORD IS SITTING
YOU MAY HAVE BEEN BRAGGING A LIFETIME OR SO
BUT NOW, WHEN IT MATTERS, YOU'RE SHITTING!

(THE ARMY *has come back just in time to hear* LILLIAN *say
   this. Gasps, which* SHE *and* BILL *don't notice*)

AH, THE SEA IS BLUE, SO BLUE
AND ALL THE WORLD GOES ON ITS WAY

BUT WHEN YOUR DAY IS OVER
THERE IS NO OTHER DAY.
AH, THE SEA IS BLUE, SO BLUE
YOU DON'T HAVE THAT LONG TO STAY
AH, THE SEA IS BLUE, SO BLUE
AH, THE SEA IS BLUE, SO BLUE
AH, THE SEA IS BLUE, SO BLUE
THE SEA IS BLUE.

HANNIBAL. Sister Lillian!

LILLIAN. (*Exhausted, calm*) Oh. Brother.

HANNIBAL. What are you doing?

LILLIAN. I was preaching a sermon to this sinner.

HANNIBAL. A sermon? To one man? What was your text?
Take off that hat, you look ridiculous. And what's that on your
breath? This is scandalous.

MARY. It really is shocking.

HANNIBAL. I'm reporting you to the Major. Shame, Lillian.

BILL. (*To* HANNIBAL) Leave her alone, creep.

HANNIBAL. (*Backing off*) And you keep out of this. You
don't have your gang of roughnecks here to threaten us now.
Come on, Lillian.

LILLIAN. (*Sadly, to* BILL) I have to go eat my grass now.

(COP *enters*)

COP. Are you Bill Cracker?

HANNIBAL. Certainly not!

BILL. I'm Cracker, Hawkshaw, what's your problem?

(LILLIAN, *feeling guilty, is hiding her head on* HANNIBAL's
shoulder)

COP. (*To* BILL) Where were you at seven o'clock this
evening?

BILL. I was here.

COP. Any witnesses?

BILL. (*Points to* LILLIAN) Her.

COP. (*Suggesting*) Just her? (BILL *nods*. COP *goes to*
LILLIAN) Miss, were you and this man alone here at seven
o'clock this evening?

LILLIAN. Seven o'clock?

COP. Just over an hour ago.

LILLIAN. Alone? Here?

HANNIBAL. (*Sotto voce*) Think of the scandal!

LILLIAN. (*Looking at* HANNIBAL) Well, I was here, and there were some others with us, and then — and then — we all left, and I just came back right now.

COP. I see. (*Going back to* BILL) Cracker, you're under arrest for the murder of Jacob Prinzmeyer, pharmacist, at seven o'clock tonight. They found your gun at the scene.

(BILL *automatically goes for his gun, can't find it, looks to back room, looks at* LILLIAN, *who looks guiltily away.* Projection: GOVERNOR *displaying* BILL's *revolver*)

BILL. So that's it. You light her cigarette, and wham!

MARY. Smoking cigarettes too!

JANE. Really, Lillian!

(HANNIBAL *and* ARMY *hustle* LILLIAN *up the stairs. At the door,* LILLIAN *stops to look back at* BILL. HE *turns away and holds up his hands;* COP *snaps handcuffs on him. Tableau. BLACKOUT. Title on screen above: INTERMISSION*)

END OF ACT I

ACT TWO

*The Canal Street Mission. Chairs, benches, a podium, a banner.
It all looks rather seedy. Upstairs, the tiny room LILLIAN,
JANE and MARY share. LILLIAN's suitcase on an iron cot.
As lights come up, the orchestra plays "March Ahead,"
rousingly. Title on screen: CANAL STREET MISSION
— HARD TIMES FOR HALLELUJAH LIL! Lights up to
reveal LILLIAN and MAJOR STONE (whom we have not seen
before), facing each other.*

MAJOR. Consorting with hardened criminals. In a tavern.
Singing disreputable songs. It's a serious matter, Lieutenant
Holiday.

LILLIAN. Major —

MAJOR. This is not the sort of thing I need just now. I'm
being asked to find a place for Sister Miriam, organize the
Christmas celebration, keep the daily prayer meeting going,
give a lecture at the Chamber of Commerce — and in the midst
of all this, I'm told that my most devoted worker is creating
scandal and ought to be dismissed. You have no right to do this
to me, Lillian. Have you any way of explaining your conduct?

LILLIAN. Major, we have to approach men like these in their
own world. We have to preach to them in their own language.
That's all I was doing.

MAJOR. (*Brightening*) I was hoping you'd be able to clarify
this for me.

LILLIAN. Major, our Jesus consorted with publicans and
sinners.

MAJOR. So He did, So He did. And all for the best. This song
you sang, it wasn't a profane song, was it? Just somewhat
couched in the vernacular, I suspect.

LILLIAN. Well, yes, you could say that.

MAJOR. I'm sure it was all right. Brother Hannibal, isn't
used to such things, you know. He's a sensitive man, sensitive
Perhaps you'll sing me a bit of it, just to be safe. Would you
mind, Sister Lillian?

LILLIAN. Not at all.

MAJOR. It's about sailors, I'm told.

LILLIAN. Yes, you see, they're drowning, and it goes like this:

(*Singing*)

THEN FOR ONCE YOU DON'T HEAR ALL THAT BIG
   TALK IN THE AIR
AND THE BIG TALKERS SUDDENLY LOOK SMALLER
AND THEY'RE DOWN ON THEIR KNEES AND
   MUMBLING ABOUT THEIR FATHER WHO'S UP
   THERE
AND THEY'RE STARTING TO WEIGH THE SINS THEIR
   SOULS MUST BEAR
AND THAT'S HOW THEY DIE
AND NOW LET ME TELL YOU A FACT THAT WE ALL
   OUGHT TO KNOW:
WHEN YOU STAND BEFORE THE THRONE WHERE
   OUR LORD IS SITTING
YOU MAY HAVE BEEN BRAGGING A LIFETIME OR SO
BUT NOW, WHEN IT MATTERS — YOU'RE WORRIED!

AH, THE SEA IS BLUE, SO BLUE
AND ALL THE WORLD GOES ON ITS WAY ...
(SHE *trails off. Spoken*)
And that's the gist of it.

MAJOR. Yes, I see. Well, that's really quite a serious song, isn't it? The last rhyme is a bit weak, but otherwise it seems just fine. No, I don't see anything wrong in that.

LILLIAN. Then I can stay?

(*A knock at the door*)

MAJOR. Excuse me a minute, Sister Lillian. (SHE *goes to the door and admits* COP) What can we do for you, officer?

COP. I'm looking for Miss Holiday.

MAJOR. Yes, she's right here.

COP. That statment you were going to write out for me, Miss.

LILLIAN. Yes, I have it right here. (*Takes it from her uniform pocket and gives it to him*)

COP. Yes . . . hm . . . good . . . wait. Miss Holiday: It says here that you *were* alone with the suspect between 6:30 and 7:30. Yesterday you told us you didn't arrive there till later. Now which is right?

LILLIAN. This is right, officer. I was alone with him for

that hour.

MAJOR. Lieutenant Holiday!

COP. Then he has an alibi for that hour.

LILLIAN. He did not commit that crime, officer. When I talked to you yesterday, I didn't know what was at stake. (*To* MAJOR) I can't let my own reputation stand in the way of the truth.

MAJOR. You know what this means, Lieutenant.

COP. You're letting the toughest crook in Chicago slip through our hands, Miss.

LILLIAN. I'm telling you the truth, officer.

COP. That's not what the Commissioner needs just now. (*Exit, disgruntled*)

MAJOR. You'd better go upstairs and pack, Lieutenant. And change out of your uniform. You're relieved of all duties. I'm sorry. Major Irving at the central office will give you your orders from now on.

LILIAN. Major, I was struggling for that man's soul.

MAJOR. I realize that, Lieutenant. But the Devil was struggling for yours as well. And it's not up to me to say who won.

(LILLIAN *turns and goes up the stairs.* HANNIBAL, BEN, MIRIAM, *now in uniform,* MARY *and* JANE *have come in during this last exchange*)

MAJOR. Sister Lillian has been relieved of her duties here. (*To* MARY & JANE) You two sisters will help her pack and receive her final notes on the sermon for tonight's meeting.

(JANE *and* MARY *follow* LILLIAN *up the stairs*)

MAJOR. Sister Miriam, you'll be able to move your belongings out of the kitchen now. You'll have Miss Holiday's old room. Meantime, will you start preparing the soup for tonight. (MIRIAM, *upset by* LILLIAN'S *ouster, looks displeased*) Brother Owens can show you how. (MIRIAM *brightens up*) Captain Jackson, you'd better help me clean the hall and pass out the hymn books. It's getting late.

HANNIBAL. (*Taking a pile of hymnbooks*) I want to be careful about overwork, Major. I'm getting the old ache in my head again.

MAJOR. All right, everybody. Get to work.

(MIRIAM & BEN *exit to the kitchen*)

JANE. (*Half-singing, on her way up the stairs*) Ah, the sea is blue, so blue . . .

MARY. . . . And pride will have a fall.

(THEY *giggle*)

LILLIAN. (*Packing upstairs, while* JANE *and* MARY *whisper to each other*) Do you want to hear the sermon or don't you?

MARY. Well, I don't know if I can preach one of those modern vernacular sermons you deliver so well. I'm not as aware of the ins and outs of progressive ideas as you are.

JANE. Did he try to kiss you?

HANNIBAL. (*Just before reaching bench*) Oh! Oh! My head! (*Collapses, scattering hymnbooks all over*)

MAJOR. Brother Hannibal! Miriam, get the smelling salts!

(MIR'AM *and* BEN *run out and help* MAJOR *rouse* HANNIBAL)

LILLIAN. (*Ignoring* JANE) I was thinking we'd make the sermon on that subject exactly. We could use the image of a radio. Like this: Lots of people today thing it's fashionable to laugh when God is mentioned, and say, "Yes, but have you ever seen Him? You can't believe in something you can't see." There's even a famous French astronomer who said, in print, "I searched with my telescope from one end of the universe to the other, and I couldn't find God."

MARY. (*Rehearsing*) "I searched with my telescope . . ."

JANE. (*Writing in a tiny notebook*) " . . . and you couldn't find God." Did he take liberties?

HANNIBAL. (*Waking up*) It started five years ago. Just before the Army took me in. I was — I was — well, I don't remember what I was, but I remember something hit me on the head, hard, and ever since then I black out occasionally.

MAJOR. How often?

HANNIBAL. Oh, not that often. (HE *immediately faints again*)

LILLIAN. Well, of course he couldn't find God. He was using the wrong instrument. You don't see God with a telescope. And here I thought we'd bring in the miracle of radio.

MARY. The radio? What does the radio have to do with it?

JANE. Did he turn the radio on?

LILLIAN. (*Very fast*) It's like this: One day, suddenly, you're told that there are waves in the air that carry sound. And you can't see them. And you don't believe they exist. Then one day

you set up a crystal set, and put on the earphones — and all
at once you hear music! And *then*, you believe.

MARY. (*Utterly confused*) The radio? Well, I suppose.

JANE. I'll bet the music was nice.

HANNIBAL. Where am I?

BEN. You had a fainting spell.

HANNIBAL. Fainting spell! It started five years ago, just
before the Army —

MAJOR. Yes, Brother, we understand. Now why don't you
go into the kitchen and relax for a while? Sister Miriam will
fix you some chicken soup.

(BEN *and* MIRIAM *walk* HANNIBAL *shakily into the kitchen.*
MAJOR *sighs and starts to pass out hymnbooks*)

LILLIAN. God is always broadcasting. His music is always on
the air. It's just a question of using the right tool, the right
part of you, to hear Him with. We can all see God in our
hearts, and hear His music in our souls: It's just a matter of
tuning in on His wave length. (SHE *has meanwhile packed her
few belongings and picked up her suitcase*) Now, do you think
you can follow all that?

MARY. Oh, yes, it seems quite simple.

JANE. I think my notes ought to help.

LILLIAN. I see the Mission is in good hands. (SHE *comes
downstairs*)

MAJOR. Well, Lillian, goodbye and good luck.

LILLIAN. Yes, I'm leaving now. I'm sure your Mission will
keep the great work going, you've got some fine workers here.
Mary's going to give a simply glowing sermon, aren't you,
darling?

HANNIBAL. (*Who has staggered to the kitchen door; weak-
ly*) Lillian, I . . .

LILLIAN. (*Turning at street door*) You hypocritical . . . stool
pigeon! (SHE *runs out, almost crying. At the same time* SAM
pokes his head in)

SAM. Begging your pardon, would this be the Salvation
Army?

JANE. I'm sorry sir. The meeting won't begin for a while.
Could you come back later?

SAM. (*Pushing right past her*) Oh, then this *is* the Salvation Army. I knew it, and you're the lovely ladies I heard singing yesterday. Don't you all have wonderful voices. And what
a charming place. (*Comes to* MAJOR) You must be the General.

General, I want to tell you, it touches my heart when I think
of the fine work your dedicated band is doing to spread a little
joy in the world. That girl who makes the speeches — now isn't
she an inspiration? Best thing I've heard since William Jennings Bryan. Magnificent!

MAJOR. I see, and you're one of the men from Bill's Beer
Hall, are you? Well, you won't find her here any longer.

SAM. Are you equating me with that lot of numbskulls and
rapscallions? Field Marshal, you've done me an injury. I'm
here on *your* behalf, and you wound me to the quick. I ought
to walk right out that door.

(JANE *holds it open for him.* HE *starts to leave, but zooms
back*)

SAM. But I can't return hurt for hurt. I couldn't leave without telling you about the joy I've come here to bring you.

MAJOR. Yes, just why have you come here?

SAM. Brigadier, have you ever rejoiced in an organ?

MAJOR. I beg your pardon?

SAM. I mean, have you ever thrilled to the sound of a great
cathedral organ?

MAJOR. Well —

SAM. Well, then you know how that passionate echoing music
stirs the crowds. As it happens, this is your lucky day, Commander. I'm prepared to offer you a fabulous bargain on an
organ. It just came into my family through an unusual set of
coincidences, it's no use to me and I'm willing to let you have it
at cost: Only four hundred dollars. Now how does that strike
you? (HE *has pulled the* MAJOR *over to one side. Meantime*
JANE *has opened the door and* THE FOLD *is starting to wander
in for the meeting: Drunks, eccentric old ladies, a few pious
farmers, a hooker, a blind man, etc.*)

MAJOR. My dear sir, we have no space for an organ here.
Look at this place.

SAM. Yes, look at this place.

MAJOR. That's just what I said.

SAM. And that's what I'm saying to you, Admiral. It's evident to my eye that you need a little zing in your business.
Don't forget the words of Henry Ford, that great man.

MAJOR. What did he say?

SAM. You don't know what he said?

MAJOR. No, what did he say?

SAM. He said: I consider every offer. Now Commodore, can

you afford to ignore the sound advice of a prominent American?

MAJOR. I really have no time to deal with this —

SAM. It has the tone of a thousand angels!

MAJOR. We're about to start our meeting —

SAM. It's a purchase you'll never regret, I promise you!

MAJOR. All right.

SAM. You'll take it?

MAJOR. Yes — no! I'll speak to you afterwards.

SAM. (*Sitting down*) Major, you've got a heart of gold.

(MAJOR *goes to the pulpit*)

MAJOR. Welcome, dear friends in Jesus. We will open our meeting tonight with Number Three in your hymnbooks, "Brother, Give Yourself a Shove."

JANE. Rise, please.

ARMY & FOLD (*Sing*)
BROTHER, GIVE YOURSELF A SHOVE
LET YOURSELF NOT WAVER
IF YOU LOVE THE LORD ABOVE
IF YOU LOVE THE LORD ABOVE
HE WILL KEEP YOU IN HIS FAVOR
BROTHER, GIVE YOURSELF A SHOVE
BROTHER, GIVE YOURSELF A SHOVE
BROTHER, GIVE YOURSELF A SHOVE.

MAJOR. Be seated.

(ALL *sit, except* ARMY OFFICERS, *who stand on either side of* MAJOR *on podium.* MAJOR *opens Bible and reads*)

MAJOR. Psalm 69. "Save me, O God, for the waters are come in unto my soul. I sink in deep mire, where there is no standing . . . "

(*While* MAJOR *reads, lights fade on Mission. Title on screen: MEANWHILE, IN THE ENEMY CAMP . . . lights slowly come up on the Beer Hall, where* BABY FACE *and* GOVERNOR *are sitting at the bar — a few stools and a bit of rail will suggest the scene*)

BABY FACE. (*Very jumpy*) Gimme one good reason!

GOVERNOR. Calm, Baby. Have drink. Whiskey heal all wound.

BABY FACE. I wanna know why.we framed Bill. He was my only friend in the gang.

GOVERNOR. You are so young. But unless you get smarter, you not live to get much older.

BABY FACE. You better give me a straight answer — or you're gonna end up under Lake Michigan, in a cement kimono!

GOVERNOR. Did you know, Baby, Fly is long time planning merger with Gorilla Baxley gang?

BABY FACE. Wha? Jeez, I didn't know that.

GOVERNOR. When Bill rub out Gorilla, is A-number-One interference.

BABY FACE. But I thought Gorilla Baxley was our competrition —

GOVERNOR. No, Gorilla was friend. Bill was big headache.

BABY FACE. But Bill was great! Bill was the toughest guy in the gang!

GOVERNOR. That is why he was big headache.

BABY FACE. (*Jumping up, waving his gun*) You're confusin' me! And when I get confused, I start shootin!

GOVERNOR. Not good to wave gat. Might hit valuable friend. (HE *karate-chops* BABY FACE's *wrist and snatches his gun*) Permit me to offer piece of ancient Oriental wisdom. (GOVERNOR *sings "SONG OF THE BIG SHOT." As* HE *sings,* HE *methodically roughs* BABY FACE *up, feinting and outmaneuvering him at every turn, in rhythm*)

GOVERNOR (*Sings*)
IF YOU WANT TO BE A BIG SHOT
START BY LEARNING TO BE TOUGH
'CAUSE YOU'LL NEVER HIT THE JACKPOT
TILL YOU LIKE THE GOING ROUGH

ALL THE LITTLE SHOTS BELOW YOU
CAN BE BLOWN AWAY LIKE FLUFF
IF THEY REALIZE WHEN THEY KNOW YOU
THAT YOU WON'T TAKE ALL THEIR GUFF

JUST DON'T GET SOFT, BABY
FOR GOD'S SAKE NEVER GET SOFT, BABY
JUST KEEP ON POUNDING HIM RIGHT WHERE IT
   HURTS THE MOST
AND IF A LITTLE SHOT'S BIG NOISE SHOULD
   CAUSE A BOTHER

DON'T LET IT GET YOU DOWN, I MEAN YOU'RE
  NOT HIS FATHER

JUST DON'T GET SOFT, BABY
FOR GOD'S SAKE NEVER GET SOFT, BABY.
NO IFS OR BUTS
GO ON AND KICK HIM IN THE GUTS
GO ON AND KICK HIM IN THE GUTS

(*Blackout on Beer Hall. Title on Screen: A SORTIE INTO
    UNKNOWN TERRITORY! Lights up on Mission*)

MAJOR. (*Finishing Psalm*) " . . . for the Lord heareth the
poor, and despiseth not His prisoners."
EVERYONE. Amen.

(BILL *comes into the Mission. The* ARMY, FOLD *and* SAM
    react)

MAJOR. And now, Sister Jane Grant will lead us in Number
Eight, "Don't Be Afraid."

(JANE *comes up to the pulpit, evidently rendered quite nervous
    by* BILL's *presence. During her song* HE *sees* SAM *at the
    back of the room and goes to him — as quietly as* HE *can,
    but nonetheless attracting a great deal of attention.* HE
    is smoking a cigarillo, for which BEN *officiously holds out
    an ashtray*)

JANE. (*Sings*)
DON'T BE AFRAID
DON'T BE AFRAID
THOUGH CORRUPTION LEADS YOU ASTRAY
GOD WILL TAKE YOU IN HIS RIGHT HAND
HE WILL SHOW YOU THE VIRTUOUS WAY
DON'T BE AFRAID
DON'T BE AFRAID
DON'T BE AFRAID

(THE FOLD *takes up the tune and hums it as* BILL *reaches
    SAM, who is very edgy.* THEY *converse in whispers*)

SAM. Hello, Bill.
BILL. Where is she?
SAM. Where is who?

BILL. That broad who gives the sermons. I gotta see her.

SAM. Oh . . . I dunno . . . I don't think she's here.

BILL. (*Louder, just as* FOLD *finishes*) What do you mean, she's not here?

MAJOR. (*Glaring at this source of noise*) That was lovely, Jane. And now (*Coldly*) if the congregation will give us their full attention, Captain Jackson will lead us all in the popular hymn, "In Our Childhood's Bright Endeavor," accompanied by chimes.

BILL. Where is she?

SAM. (*Frantic*) How do I know?

MAJOR. Are you distressed, brothers? Can we be of some help to you?

SAM. (*Seizing his chance*) I really must be going, Major — pressing business — thank you for everything — you've changed my life — goodbye — bless you —(*Exits quickly, tripping over podium*)

MAJOR. (*To* BILL) And you, brother? Can we be of help to you?

BILL. I don't know.

MAJOR. Perhaps you'll stay and pray with us?

BILL. I might stick around, at that.

MAJOR. Very good. (*Going back to pulpit*) Brother Jackson, if you will oblige.

HANNIBAL. (*Sings*)
IN OUR CHILDHOOD'S BRIGHT ENDEAVOR
WE WERE WARMED IN MOTHER'S ARMS
NOW THAT WARMTH IS GONE FOREVER
LIKE OUR CHILDHOOD'S FADING CHARMS

MARY. (*Whispering*) Major, that's the man they found with Sister Lillian!

MAJOR. (*Her face clouding over*) I see.

HANNIBAL. (*After clearing his throat to quiet them*)
BUT THE SOUND OF CHURCH BELLS TOLLING
THROUGH OUR PAIN AND OUR DISMAY
SO INSPIRING, SO CONSOLING —
THEY ARE TOLLING STILL TODAY

(*Lights down on Mission, up on bar.* LILLIAN *enters*)

LILLIAN. Excuse me — where's Mr. Cracker?

GOVERNOR. (*Smiling*) Mr. Cracker out to lunch. For about twenty year.

LILLIAN. Oh, that's not true.

BABY FACE. Girlie, wasn't you here when they took him away?

LILLIAN. Yes.

BABY FACE. So there must be something wrong with your head. He's in jail. Where did you think they was taking him, the Palmer House?

LILLIAN. But they let him out. He's free.

(BABY FACE *and* GOVERNOR *look at each other in consternation*)

LILLIAN. I told them the truth, that he was here with me when that man was killed. So I'll just wait . . .

GOVERNOR. Not wise, Miss Holiday Lil.

(SAM *runs in, breathless*)

SAM. They let him out! He's free! He's on the loose!

LILLIAN. Where is he?

SAM. The Salvation Army, Canal Street.

(LILLIAN *starts to run out;* BABY FACE *grabs her*)

BABY FACE. Hold on, Sister Salvation, you ain't going no place.

GOVERNOR. You watch her, Baby Face. I take care of Mr. Cracker. (GOVERNOR *exits, gun drawn.* SAM *swigs from his flask. Lights down on Beer Hall and up on Mission*)

MAJOR. And now, dear friends, our own Lieutenant Mary Pritchard will preach to you on the topic, "God Is on the Air Waves."

MARY. Thank you, Major. You know, ladies and gentlemen, a lot of people think you can't see God. (*Long pause*) Well, and of course you can't. You don't see God, you hear Him . . . No, that's not what I mean . . .

(*Pause.* JANE *is miming "telescope"*)

Oh, yes, telescope! Thank you, Jane. Yes, people think you can't see God. A famous French astronomer actually wrote a letter to his telescope — I mean, he wrote a letter to a newspaper and said, "I took my telescope, and I sort of poked around the whole world, but I couldn't see God." Well, of course not. (*Pause*)

A VOICE IN THE CONGREGATION. Where's Lillian?

MARY. You don't see God just because you have a telescope. It's not the right tool. But you can see Him if the right tool comes to hand.

(*Snickers in the audience*)

I mean, what you need is a radio. I mean, God isn't on the radio, but —

MORE VOICES. (*Stamping feet, pounding, hooting, etc.*) We want Lillian! Where's Lillian! Where's the Hallelujah girl!

MARY. (*Desperately shouting over the clamor*) — but if you use your ears, you can see Him! I mean, for Christ's sake, He broadcasts every hour!

A LOT OF VOICES. LILLIAN! Lillian! We want Lillian!

BILL. (*Jumping up*) Yeah. Let's have Lillian Holiday! I got something to say to her. Where's she hiding?

MAJOR. (*Topping all the clamor, sternly*) We will not be going on with this service until we have silence. (THEY *quiet down*) Thank you for your brave effort, Sister Mary. (MARY *retires from the podium, biting her lip*) This is the House of the Lord, brothers and sisters. Aren't you ashamed to confront Him with such behaviour? Now, as Miss Holiday won't be with us this evening —

BILL. Why won't she?

MAJOR. Miss Holiday has been dismissed from our service, Mr. Cracker. And you of all people should know the reasons. Now, as she won't be here, we'll continue our meeting with —

BILL. (*Starting for the* MAJOR) Why, you cheesy crumb-bun — (HE *is about to grab* MAJOR *when* GOVERNOR *comes in, gun draw*n)

GOVERNOR. Excuse me! I hope I am not interrupting. No one move, please.

(HANNIBAL *drops to the floor in a faint.* JANE *goes to revive him*)

GOVERNOR. Just go on with your service. I see Mr. Cracker have been causing more trouble, but not to worry: He will soon be out of your way. (*Dead silence*) Please to continue, Major.

MAJOR. — that beloved temperance ballad, "The Liquor Dealer's Dream."

GOVERNOR. One of my favorites!

MAJOR. Captain Jackson?

(*Title on screen: THE LIQUOR DEALER'S DREAM.* HAN-
NIBAL, *who has gotten shakily to his feet, moves toward
the podium, tries to change his mind and go back, is
brought down to the podium again. Meantime,* BILL, *hands
high, has made his way over to* GOVERNOR'S *side in re-
sponse to* GOVERNOR'S *waves of gun*)

HANNIBAL. (*Sings*)

AT THE BAR, BEHIND A PILE OF GLASSES
BLEARY-EYED, WITH PUFFY PURPLE LIPS
SLEEPS A PALE AND SWEATY LIQUOR DEALER
TROUSERS BULGING ON HIS FLABBY HIPS
AND HE DREAMS THAT HE'S GONE TO HEAVEN
AND HE'S CALLED TO THE JUDGMENT BOARD
AND HE SLUGS DOWN SCOTCH IN A FRENZY
TILL HE'S DRUNKER THAN A LORD

ALL. (GOVERNOR *conducts with his gun*)

THROW OUT THE LIFELINE! SOUL OVERBOARD!
THROW OUT THE LIFELINE! SOUL OVERBOARD!

HANNIBAL AND GOVERNOR. (GOVERNOR *moves over to har-
monize with* HANNIBAL, *who gets more frantic with each note.
In* GOVERNOR'S *enjoyment of song,* HE *occasionally points pistol at* HANNIBAL'S *head instead of* BILL'S)

AND HIS KNOCKING KNEES GIVE WAY BENEATH
   HIM
AND HE SEES NO HELP: HE'S DOOMED TO FAIL
AND HE FEELS THE SWORD ABOVE HIS NECKBONE
AND HIS SHIRT, THAT'S DAMP FROM TOP TO TAIL
AND HE SHAMES HIMSELF IN TERROR
THERE BEFORE ALL THE HEAVENLY HOST
AND HE THINKS, "BECAUSE I SELL SPIRITS
GOD HAS GIVEN UP MY GHOST."

ALL.

THROW OUT THE LIFELINE! SOUL OVERBOARD!
THROW OUT THE LIFELINE! SOUL OVERBOARD!

(HANNIBAL *has fainted at end of second verse;* ALL *sing
chorus while staring at him.* GOVERNOR *picks out* JANE,

*who is kneeling over him, and with his revolver motions
her to get up and sing. During her verse,* HE *waves goodbye jauntily and marches* BILL *out the front door at gun-
point)*

JANE.
THEN HE WAKES: HIS BLEARY EYES ARE STARING
AND THE PURPLE'S PALER ON HIS LIPS
AND HE SAYS, "I'VE GOT TO MEND MY WAYS NOW,"
HIKES HIS PANTS UP ON HIS FLABBY HIPS,
"AND TO WIDOWS AND ORPHAN CHILDREN
"TO THE NEEDY, THE OLD, THE POOR,
"I WILL DONATE THIS DIRTY MONEY
"THAT HAS MADE MY SOUL IMPURE."

*(*GOVERNOR *and* BILL *disappear. Sounds of scuffle. Gunshot.
Splash.* EVERYONE *quails while singing)*

ALL.
SOUL SAFELY RESCUED!
SOUL SAFELY RESCUED!

*(*BILL *comes back in with the gun.* EVERYONE *gasps)*

BILL. Don't mind me, I'm just passing through—out the
back window. I hope you'll be so good as to sing that last
chorus again whilst I takes my leave. Just act natural. *(*HE
points gun at ARMY. *While* GROUP *sings,* HE *crosses the room,
climbs the stairs, and exits out upstairs window)*

ALL.
SOUL SAFELY RESCUED!
SOUL SAFELY RESCUED!

LILLIAN. *(Appearing at front door just in time to see* BILL
disappear out window) Bill!

*(*EVERYONE *whirls around and gapes at* LILLIAN. *Tableau.
Blackout)*

END OF ACT II

ACT III

SCENE 1

Bill's Beer Hall. Orchestra plays "BILBAO SONG." Title on screen: CHRISTMAS EVE!

> *As lights come up, THE GANG, minus SAM and GOVERNOR, are assembled in the beer hall preparing for the robbery. BILL is pacing; THE OTHERS are watching the PROFESSOR work on an extravagant machine, on one of the tables, that resembles a cross between a telegraph and a radio, with a large gramophone horn on top. Music out.*

REVEREND. What are you doing there, inventing the wheel?

PROFESSOR. Go peddle your snake oil!

BILL. Come on, Marconi, shake a leg.

PROFESSOR. Leave me be, willya? I gotta get the carbon diode hooked up to the generator.

BABY FACE. Yeah, he's gotta get the carbon diode hooked up to the —

BILL. Button it!

PROFESSOR. What a thing to leave to the last minute! If the Governor was here we'da' been organized.

BABY FACE. Yeah, if the Governor was here we'd —

(BILL *starts to move toward him*)

— we'd — we'd haveta split the take six ways instead of five.

(SAM *flounces on, grotesquely dressed as a woman*)

SAM. Reverend! You forgot to get me the goddam hairpins!

GANG. (*Ad lib whistles, exlamations, etc.*) Oh, Mammy!

PROFESSOR. Well, aren't you the monkey's instep!

SAM. You like it, huh, boys? Of course, I don't know if I like it — an artist is never satisfied! Tell me, Baby Face, will it make the coppers think I'm your dear old mother?

BABY FACE. Gee, I dunno. My mother was a blonde.
REVEREND. And we can all testify to that!

(*General uproar.* SAM *wiggles gleefully*)

BILL. Shake that moneymaker, sweetheart. Gentlemen, Bill's Beer and Music Hall proudly presents the Queen of the Loop — Mammy Wurlitzer!
SAM. (*High tragedy*) Like that old dame says in the play: "You can do whatever you like to me — but I'll still be Mother Goddam!"

(*Title on screen: THE MANDALAY SONG*)

SAM. (*Sings*)
MOTHER GODDAM'S DIVE IN MANDALAY
SEVEN ROTTEN BOARDS OUT ON THE BAY
GODDAM, GO TELL THAT GIRL TO GET HER ASS
   IN GEAR
THERE'S FIFTEEN GUYS ALREADY LINED UP
   ALONG THE PIER
WATCHES IN THEIR HANDS AND SHOUTING "HEY!"
"IS THERE JUST ONE GIRL IN MANDALAY?"

ALL THE GIRLS ARE CUTE AS THEY CAN BE
EVEN IF THEY WON'T PUT OUT FOR FREE!
LIFE WOULD BE SO SIMPLE
EVERYTHING IN ORDER
IF THE GUY WHO'S IN THERE
WASN'T SO DAMN SLOW
TAKE YOUR FORTY-FIVE AND SHOOT THE DOOR
   DOWN
TELL THAT GUY IN THERE HE'S HOLDING UP THE
   SHOW
FASTER JOHNNY, HEY
FASTER JOHNNY, HEY
SING THE MAN THE SONG OF MANDALAY

ALL. (*Sing*)
LOVE DOESN'T HAVE DAYS AND WEEKS TO BE
   RECKONED
JOHNNY, COME ON, DON'T YOU DARE WASTE A
   SECOND

WILL THE MOON SHINE EVERY NIGHT OVER YOU,
  MANDALAY?
WILL THE MOON SHINE EVERY NIGHT OVER YOU?

SAM.
MOTHER GODDAM'S DIVE IN MANDALAY
NOW IT'S ROTTING UNDERNEATH THE BAY
GODDAM, THAT GIRL IN THERE CAN REST HER
  LITTLE REAR
THERE'S NOT A SINGLE CLIENT OUT WAITING
  ON THE PIER
NO MORE WATCHES LEFT, NO SHOUTS OF, "HEY!"
NOT A SINGLE SOUL IN MANDALAY . . .

ONCE THE GIRLS WERE CUTE AS THEY COULD BE
NOW THERE'S NOT A ONE THAT'S WORTH HER FEE!
LIFE'S NO LONGER SIMPLE
NOTHING IS IN ORDER
THERE'S NO PLACE LIKE GODDAM'S
ALL OF THEM ARE GONE.
NO MORE FORTY-FIVES TO SHOOT THE DOOR DOWN
WHERE THERE'S NO ONE — THE SHOW JUST CAN'T
  GO ON.
FASTER JOHNNY, HEY
FASTER JOHNNY, HEY
SING THE MAN THE SONG OF MANDALAY

ALL.
LOVE DOESN'T HAVE DAYS AND WEEKS TO BE
  RECKONED
JOHNNY, COME ON, DON'T YOU DARE WASTE A
  SECOND
WILL THE MOON SHINE EVERY NIGHT OVER YOU,
  MANDALAY?
WILL THE MOON SHINE EVERY NIGHT OVER YOU?

(*Uproarious laughter and hi-jinks, suddenly* PROFESSOR's *ma-
    chine gives a small explosion, then starts to sputter and
    spark*)

VOICE OF THE FLY. (*Out of gramophone horn*) Hello. Hello.
The Fly is on the wing.
PROFESSOR. We got it! It's working!

(THEY *all gather round machine*)

PROFESSOR. Johnny, c'mere and help me with this. (BABY FACE *comes closer*) Turn this wheel. Very slowly. Now, when I get these two wires together . . . Slowly, slowly . . . Ow! Wait stop! Stop! (*Pulls his finger out of wiring*) Oo, you really gave me a shock. All right, try it again. (BABY FACE *turns wheel. Machine begins to give off static*)

SAM. Fantastic!

FLY's VOICE. All right, boys! Here are the assignments for tonight's caper: The place is the Manufacturer's National Bank.

(*Ad libs of delights from* GANG)

FLY's VOICE. Thought you'd like that. Professor.

(PROFESSOR *starts to say something*)

FLY's VOICE. Don't interrupt! At 10:15 you'll park the car on Division Street, cut around the alley to the back entrance, and kill the alarm system. Mammy and Baby Face, mother and son as usual. Mammy covers the front entrance. Baby slips in the back way and knocks out the night watchman.

SAM. You got that, Baby Face?

FLY's VOICE. Don't ask stupid questions, you'll confuse him. Reverend will come down Clark Street, reconnoiter with Mammy at 10:23, and get the acetylene torch from him.

BILL. And be on time, dimwit.

FLY's VOICE. Butt out, Bill. We don't need a repetition of yesterday's incident. Remember, you're still on probation. Now then: Sam will bring the car around to the alleyway. The rest of you yo-yos will meet him there at 10:35. Meantime Bill comes up the alley from the other side, picks up the bundle, and goes off in the opposite direction. And you better make good, Bill. Remember, if we can do without the Governor, we can do without you . . .

(*This last sentence comes out a bit distorted, as* BABY FACE, *in his nervousness for* BILL, *turns the wheel more and more slowly.* BILL *makes a derisive gesture at the machine*)

FLY's VOICE. I saw that!

(EVERYONE *does a take*)

FLY's VOICE. All right, I'll meet you clowns back here at

eleven. Synchronize watches. The time now is 9:14. (*Electronic beep.* THEY ALL *start to head out*) Hold it, jerks!

(THEY ALL *stop dead*)

FLY's VOICE. Your alibis are in that bottle on the bar. Ten seconds to learn them. Oh, and boys — Merry Christmas.

(*Ad libs of "Merry Christmas" back*)

FLY's VOICE. This is the Fly buzzing off!

(*Static. Machine goes dead.* BILL *finds the alibi slips, passes them out*)

PROFESSOR. (*Reading*) "Ten till midnight, Hinky Dink Saloon. Witnesses: Tessie Miller, Eddie the Bartender." Aw, not Tessie Miller.

(BILL *gives him a dirty look.* HE *shuts up*)

SAM. "Cab ride to Forest Park, Yellow Cab number 35259. Witness: Cab driver, Steve Lardner, 111 North Clark." What was I doing in Forest Park? Oh, well.
BABY FACE & REVEREND. (*Overlapping* SAM's *last line*) "Birthday party at Captain Wolf's. Intimate dinner — (THEY *realize their slips are identical*) with relatives. All evening. Sixty East Oak Street. Witnesses: Wolf family.
BILL. (*Who has looked at his, nodded, and declined to read it aloud*) Have we got 'em?

(ALL *ad lib agreement*)

BILL. Get rid of 'em.

(ALL *eat alibi slips,* REVEREND *spitting his*)

PROFESSOR. (*Swallowing*) Ugh.
BILL. Okay, now beat it while your shoes are still good.

(THE GANG, *impressed by his commanding manner, packs up quickly*)

SAM. Looks like Bill's right back in charge.

BABY FACE. Yeah, we was really worried about you. I thought you was gonna turn this place into another Holy Army mission.

(BILL *glares at them. Behind his back, the machine suddenly explodes.* HE *whirls, gun drawn, sees what it is, puts gun away*)

REVEREND. (*Begins to sing, softly*) "Oh, holy night, the stars is brightly shining . . . "

(THE GANG *takes it up, laughing, as* THEY *run up the stairs*)

BILL. (*Over this*) All right, out, out, all of youse!

(*Lights dim.* BILL *pours himself a drink and sits morosely, his back to the door. Title on screen: THE DESPAIR OF A LONELY CRIMINAL . . .*)

BILL. Goddam it.

(*2nd Title on screen: . . . IS MATCHED BY THE SORROW OF A DOWNCAST SAINT . . .*)

LILLIAN *enters, carrying her suitcase.* BILL *does not turn around*)

BILL. We're closed.

(SHE *comes down the steps*)

BILL. I said we're closed. (HE *turns around*) Oh . . . it's you.
LILLIAN. I've left the Army, and I have no place to go in the meantime. So I thought I'd just see how you were getting along.
BILL. Well, that's real nice of you, but I'm busy. And you can't stay here, so you better go.
LILLIAN. (*Seating herself at the bar*) You're not busy, Mr. Cracker. And I'm not going.
BILL. How do you know I'm not busy, Miss Holiday? What do you know about my life?
LILLIAN. I've seen it. I've seen through it. I saw what you did to that poor Japanese man yesterday.
BILL. Yeah, and did you see what he was gonna do to me?

I just did it to him first, that's all.

LILLIAN. I didn't set you free so you could do that.

BILL. Set me free? Listen, where the hell do you get off, thinkin' you can make the world so much better than it is? I coulda hired a dozen broads to tell the cops what you told them.

LILLIAN. They wouldn't have been telling the truth.

BILL. The truth? Who cares about the truth? Since when do you carry keys to the slammer?

LILLIAN. They had you up for murder — and they let you out because they trusted me.

BILL. And when I got out I killed a guy. See, you had me all wrong.

LILLIAN. Aren't you even sorry?

BILL. Sorry? Yeah — I'm sorry I didn't get his hat for my collection.

LILLIAN. Is that all?

BILL. All? Oh, wait a minute. You mean, am I sorry you lost your job? Well, listen, sister, it ain't my fault, if Jesus fired you cause he's got a dirty mind.

LILLIAN. Jesus didn't fire me. Jesus is still with me.

BILL. Great, then what're you bothering me for? Why don't you go home and keep Him happy?

LILLIAN. I'm not worried about His happiness. I'm worried about yours.

BILL. I'm happy! I'm as happy as I can be! Open your eyes, why don't you? Take a look around you! Do you know where you are?

LILLIAN. Bill's Beer Hall.

BILL. Bill's Beer Hall, and I'm Bill. I run this place. I make good money out of what goes on here, which is none of your damn business so we won't talk about it — and you know what happens when I go outside?

LILLIAN. No.

BILL. Every man, woman, and child in the 43rd Ward says, "There goes Bill Cracker," and they touches their hats to me.

LILLIAN. They're afraid of you.

BILL. Yeah. And that makes me feel just great. I'm on my own. I got everything I want. And nobody ever gets in my way. P.S.: I can have any broad in Chicago. So what have I got to be unhappy about?

LILLIAN. I don't know. Why are you unhappy?

BILL. I ain't! And I don't need an unemployed hallelujah tootsie telling me how to run my life.

LILLIAN. You think that's all there is to me.

BILL. I don't see nothin' else.

LILLIAN. You don't think a woman can suffer like a man.

BILL. I don't care if she does.

LILLIAN. You do care. But you want to believe you don't care.

BILL. Try me.

LILLIAN. I'll make you care. I've got a song I want you to hear.

BILL. Can I get you a hat?

LILLIAN. I don't need one.

(*Title on screen: SURABAYA JOHNNY.*)

LILLIAN. (*Sings*)
I HAD JUST TURNED SIXTEEN THAT SEASON
WHEN YOU CAME UP FROM BURMA TO STAY
AND YOU TOLD ME I OUGHT TO TRAVEL WITH YOU
YOU WERE SURE IT WOULD BE OKAY
WHEN I ASKED HOW YOU MADE YOUR LIVING
I CAN STILL HEAR WHAT YOU SAID TO ME:
YOU HAD SOME KIND OF JOB WITH THE RAILWAY
AND HAD NOTHING TO DO WITH THE SEA

YOU SAID A LOT, JOHNNY
ALL ONE BIG LIE, JOHNNY
YOU CHEATED ME BLIND, JOHNNY, FROM THE
    MINUTE WE MET
I HATE YOU SO, JOHNNY
WHEN YOU STAND THERE GRINNING, JOHNNY
TAKE THAT DAMN PIPE OUT OF YOUR MOUTH,
    YOU RAT!

SURABAYA JOHNNY, NO ONE'S MEANER THAN YOU
SURABAYA JOHNNY, MY GOD, AND I STILL LOVE
    YOU SO!
SURABAYA JOHNNY, WHY'M I FEELING SO BLUE?
YOU HAVE NO HEART, JOHNNY, AND I STILL LOVE
    YOU SO!

AT THE START EVERY DAY WAS SUNDAY
TILL WE WENT ON OUR WAY ONE FINE NIGHT
AND BEFORE TWO MORE WEEKS WERE OVER
YOU THOUGHT NOTHING I DID WAS RIGHT

SO WE TREKKED UP AND DOWN THROUGH
    THE PUNJAB
FROM THE SOURCE OF THE RIVER TO THE SEA:
WHEN I LOOK AT MY FACE IN THE MIRROR
THERE'S AN OLD WOMAN STARING BACK AT ME.

YOU DIDN'T WANT LOVE, JOHNNY
YOU WANTED CASH, JOHNNY
BUT I SAW YOUR LIPS, JOHNNY
AND THAT WAS THAT.
YOU WANTED IT ALL, JOHNNY
I GAVE YOU MORE, JOHNNY.
TAKE THAT DAMN PIPE OUT OF YOUR MOUTH,
    YOU RAT.

SURABAYA JOHNNY, NO ONE'S MEANER THAN YOU
SURABAYA JOHNNY, MY GOD, AND I STILL LOVE
    YOU SO!
SURABAYA JOHNNY, WHY'M I FEELING SO BLUE?
YOU HAVE NO HEART, JOHNNY, AND I STILL LOVE
    YOU SO!

THOUGH YOUR NAME SHOULD HAVE TOLD ME
    DIFFERENT
I HAD HOPED WE WOULD SOON SETTLE DOWN
BUT IN EVERY SALOON ON THE COASTLINE
THEY WOULD CHEER WHEN YOU CAME TO TOWN
AND ONE DAY IN A TWO-BIT FLOPHOUSE
I'LL WAKE UP TO THE ROAR OF THE SEA
AND YOU'LL LEAVE WITHOUT ONE WORD OF
    WARNING
ON THE SHIP WAITING DOWN AT THE KEY

YOU HAVE NO HEART, JOHNNY
YOU'RE JUST A LOUSE, JOHNNY
HOW CAN YOU GO, JOHNNY
AND LEAVE ME FLAT?
YOU'RE STILL MY LOVE, JOHNNY
LIKE THE DAY WE MET, JOHNNY
TAKE THAT DAMN PIPE OUT OF YOUR MOUTH,
    YOU RAT.

SURABAYA JOHNNY, NO ONE'S MEANER THAN YOU
SURABAYA JOHNNY, MY GOD, AND I STILL LOVE
    YOU SO!

SURABAYA JOHNNY, WHY'M I FEELING SO BLUE?
YOU HAVE NO HEART, JOHNNY, AND I STILL LOVE
  YOU SO!

(BILL *is crying. Neither* HE *nor* LILLIAN *notices that during
  the song* THE FLY, *disguised as a newsboy, has come in
  quietly through the back door*)

LILLIAN. You see, Bill, you do care.
BILL. Like hell I do! And even if I do, so what!

(HE *sings*)
IF YOU WANT TO BE A BIG SHOT
START BY LEARNING TO BE TOUGH
'CAUSE YOU'LL NEVER HIT THE JACKPOT
TILL YOU LIKE THE GOING ROUGH
ALL THE LITTLE SHOTS BELOW YOU
CAN BE BLOWN AWAY LIKE FLUFF
IF THEY REALIZE WHEN THEY KNOW YOU
THAT YOU WON'T TAKE ALL THEIR GUFF

JUST DON'T GET SOFT, BABY
FOR GOD'S SAKE NEVER GET SOFT, BABY
JUST KEEP ON POUNDING THEM RIGHT WHERE
  IT HURTS THE MOST
BECAUSE A BIG SHOT LIVES WITHOUT ALL THOSE
  EMOTIONS
SO YOU CAN'T KNOCK HIM DOWN WITH
  SENTIMENTAL NOTIONS
JUST DON'T GET SOFT, BABY
FOR GOD'S SAKE NEVER GET SOFT, BABY
NO IFS OR BUTS
GO ON AND KICK HIM IN THE GUTS
GO ON AND KICK HIM IN THE GUTS

(BILL *drained, wheels away from* LILLIAN, *and sees* FLY)

FLY. Got a light?
BILL. Fly! Ten-thirty!
LILLIAN. What's wrong? Who's this boy?
BILL. Eleven o'clock! It's all over, isn't it?
FLY. It sure is.
LILLIAN. Bill, what's he saying?
FLY. I want a light for my cigarette.

BILL. (*Striking a match*) Sure, sure, yes, a light. (*Match won't ignite*) Light your own damn cigarette! (*Gets up abruptly and runs out*)

LILLIAN. Bill!

FLY. And you take your cheap suitcase and get out of here.

LILLIAN. Yes, I'm going. This is no place for me. I'm going back to the Salvation Army. Maybe they'll let me start at the bottom and work my way up again. They wouldn't dare throw me out: it's Christmas. I wish I knew what I've done. (*Exit* LILLIAN. THE FLY *has changed back into female costume.* SHE *turns out the lights and waits in the dark. Orchestra plays the "MANDALAY SONG," while on the screen is shown a film sequence, or a rapid sequence of slides showing the* GANG *performing all the steps in the robbery, as described in* FLY'*s instructions. The last two shots show the money, waiting untended in the alley, and the* GANG, *piled into their car and heading back to the Beer Hall, all smiles. As the music ends* THEY *burst in, turn on lights*)

SAM. Boy oh boy oh boy! Fifty grand!

BABY FACE. Bill! Hey, Bill!

PROFESSOR. I'm gonna get me a lab that makes Menlo Park look like a phone booth!

REVEREND. Well, where is he?

BABY FACE. Bill!

SAM. (*To* PROFESSOR, *as* OTHER TWO *hunt for* BILL) I'm gonna buy a yacht as big as a cathedral!

PROFESSOR. And install your organ on it.

SAM. Right!

BARY FACE. (*In back room*) Bill!

PROFESSOR. Every fish in the lake will go deef.

(SAM *takes a playful swipe at* PROFESSOR: BABY FACE *interrupts them*)

BABY FACE. Hey, Bill ain't here!

REVEREND. It seems our pie in the sky has flown the coop.

SAM. But didn't you see him out there?

PROFESSOR. No, there was nobody in the alley but a goddam newsboy.

SAM. But our fifty grand!

REVEREND. We'll never see a penny of it now!

FLY. (*Rising from behind the bar*) Guess again. It's right here.

ALL. Fly!

PROFESSOR. You was the newsboy!

FLY. Damn straight.

SAM. (*Going for the money*) Fifty grand! Come on Mammy!

(THE OTHERS *elbow in for their share of the money;* FLY
   pushes them off)

FLY. Hold it! There's a little job to be done before we divvy
up the boodle.

REVEREND. What kind of job?

FLY. Mr. Bill Cracker.

PROFESSOR. That's right. Why didn't he show?

FLY. Mr. Cracker was preoccupied with affairs of the heart.
So he left our fifty grand slip his mind while a Salvation Army
lassie sang him an anthem or two.

SAM. I don't believe it.

FLY. I saw it.

SAM. I believe it.

FLY. So I asked him for a light.

(ALL *react*)

And this time I meant it. He knows all our plans and he's gone
soft in the head over his religious sweetie. He may be in some
little booth right now, telling some mackerel snapper all about
us. And it's only one step from the confessional to the phone
booth.

BABY FACE. Hey, we're in trouble.

FLY. Kee-rect, genius. Unless we shut his mouth before he
opens it.

BABY FACE. Wow, when I think of Bill selling out — I just
want to roll over and die.

FLY. Easy, Buster Brown. Don't start singing the blues just
yet. There's no electric cord plugged into your chair.

(SAM *has surreptitiously started fondling the money*)

FLY. And you keep your paws off! Nobody gets a cent of
that till Bill is out of the way!

REVEREND. The money means nothing! Either we get him
tonight or we have a one-way ticket to Hell tomorrow.

FLY. Just take care of business tonight. Tomorrow can take
care of itself. Tomorrow, hmmph!

(Lights change. Title on screen: BALLAD OF THE LILY OF
HELL. Projections of houseflies, enormously magnified,
seen as if through red flames. FLY *sings)*

FLY.
YOU GUYS MAY NOT BE INCLINED TO WORRY IF I
    BURN IN HELL
IF A CHICKEN SOAKED IN WINE WILL COOK TO
    MEDIUM OR WELL
IF A CHICKEN SOAKED IN WINE WILL COOK TO
    MEDIUM OR WELL
YOU GUYS MAY NOT BE INCLINED TO WORRY IF I
    BURN IN HELL
GET THIS STRAIGHT:

THAT'S A PROBLEM FOR TOMORROW
I DON'T NEED TO BORROW SORROW
T'MORROW'S NOTHING, TO BE BLUNT
YOU CAN SHOVE IT WHERE YOU WANT!

TIPS ON TOMORROW NEVER PAY
TOMORROW YOU'LL REGRET WHAT YOU DID TODAY
AND SOON ENOUGH YOU'LL BURN FOR IT AS WELL...
SO WHO GIVES A HOOT IN HELL?
—Shove tomorrow where you want!

NOW I BET YOU GUYS ARE THINKING I WANT YOU
    TO BE CONCERNED
CATCH ME WHEN YOU SEE ME SINKING, SAVE ME
    SO I DON'T GET BURNED
CATCH ME WHEN YOU SEE ME SINKING, SAVE ME
    SO I DON'T GET BURNED
YEAH, I BET YOU GUYS ARE THINKING I WANT YOU
    TO BE CONCERNED
GET THIS STRAIGHT:

I'LL TAKE CARE OF THAT TOMORROW
YOU DON'T NEED TO BORROW SORROW
T'MORROW'S NOTHING, TO BE BLUNT
YOU CAN SHOVE IT WHERE YOU WANT

TIPS ON TOMORROW NEVER PAY
TOMORROW YOU'LL REGRET WHAT YOU DID TODAY
AND SOON ENOUGH YOU'LL BURN FOR IT AS WELL...

SO WHO GIVES A HOOT IN HELL?
—Shove tomorrow where you want!

BABY FACE. (*After song*) Don't worry, Fly, we'll get him for you.
FLY. Thanks, boys. I don't know what this gang's coming to . . .

(THE GANG *starts to exit up steps but slows down to listen as* SHE *solioquizes on*)

FLY. The Governor gone and Bill pulling these crazy stunts behind my back. You boys are all I've got. I don't want to see this operation fall apart . . . the gang's meant everything to me since my man disappeared five years ago . . . What am I getting so sentimental about! If I'm not careful *I'll* be the next one into the church! (SHE *sees them clustered on the steps*) Cut the stalling! Get out of here and find that sacred-heart bastard!

(THEY *hurry out. Lights dim to a spot on her and* SHE *looks straight out at the audience, and sing*s)

FLY.
WHEN THEY COUNT MY SINS IN HEAVEN, THEN
    I'LL GET TO KNOW MY LUCK
IS IT FURNACE NUMBER SEVEN OR A HARP FOR
    ME TO PLUCK?
IS IT FURNACE NUMBER SEVEN OR A HARP FOR
    ME TO PLUCK?
WHEN THEY COUNT MY SINS IN HEAVEN, THEN
    I'LL GET TO KNOW MY LUCK
GOT THAT STRAIGHT?

LIKE I SAID, I'LL KNOW TOMORROW
I DON'T NEED TO BORROW SORROW
T'MORROW'S NOTHING, TO BE BLUNT
YOU CAN SHOVE IT WHERE YOU WANT!

TIPS ON TOMORROW NEVER PAY
TOMORROW YOU'LL REGRET WHAT YOU DID TODAY
AND SOON ENOUGH YOU'LL BURN FOR IT AS WELL . . .
SO WHO GIVES A HOOT IN HELL?

—Shove tomorrow where you want!

(Blackout. In the darkness the Orchestra plays "Don't Be Afraid" through the scene change. Lights up on Salvation Army Mission. Title on screen: ASK AND YE SHALL RECEIVE.)

ACT III

Scene 2

The Salvation Army. A mangy Christmas tree. A few of The Fold *sitting around.* Lillian *comes in and sits with them.* Jane *and* Hannibal *come in with a tureen of soup and start to ladle it out.* Jane *notices* Lillian *and points her out to* Hannibal.

Hannibal. The nerve!

Jane. Comes in and just sits down with the others. I'm going to tell the Major. *(She goes into the kitchen)*

Hannibal. Unbelievable.

Mary. *(Goes to Lillian)* Miss Holiday, I was told if you ever came back, I should ask you to please leave the premises at once. Major's orders.

Lillian. Oh? Give the Major my regards and tell her I am only a poor soul too.

(Mary turns to leave in a huff, and meets the Major coming out of the kitchen. She starts to say something, but Major cuts her off)

Major. So! . . . Well, Holiday, it seems that Bill's Beer Hall wasn't quite right for you either, hm?

(Lillian says nothing)

Well, but you really can't stay here, you know.

Mary. She says she's a poor soul too.

Major. Well, she may be a poor soul. But there are some souls we just don't want here.

LILLIAN. I was the best soldier this Army ever had. I knew how to bring God into this — this crummy joint.

(BILL *comes in, slightly drunk*)

MAJOR. And here is another example of the kind of soul we don't want.

BILL. Why, Major, it's Christmas Eve, ain't it? Bless you all, brothers and sisters. You wouldn't turn me out on a night like this — not when I'm just getting interested in what you got to offer.

MAJOR. Mr. Cracker —

LILLIAN. Of course you can stay, Bill.

MAJOR. I think that's quite enough from you, Miss Holiday.

LILLIAN. I don't think it's enough at all, Major. I don't think anything in this room is enough. What is the matter with you people? Where are your minds? There's supposed to be more joy in Heaven over one sinner's repentance than over a thousand righteous men. Here's an important sinner — and all you can give him is a cold shoulder on Christmas Eve!

MAJOR. I'm afraid, Miss Holiday, that Mr. Cracker isn't here tonight to help us pass out the Christmas presents. I don't know why he *is* here, but I know I don't want him here, or you, or the rest of his gang, so if you will kindly —

(SHE *is interrupted by* THE GANG *swaggering in*)

SAM. Merry Christmas, everybody!

MAJOR. Gentlemen, what can we do for you?

BABY FACE. We just thought we'd stop by and see how the festivities was getting along.

REVEREND. Say, that's a handsome tree, isn't it, Professor?

PROFESSOR. Sheds like a sick Pekinese!

LILLIAN. Gentlemen, I'm truly delighted to see you all here. We had a feeling you'd come, didn't we, Major? And now I think we can start our meeting.

BABY FACE. Hold it, sister. Ya see, the real reason we come by was to find a friend of ours that we ain't seen in a long time. (HE *goes to* BILL, *who has unobtrusively wandered off into a corner*) We missed you a lot tonight, buddy boy.

BILL. Missed me?

REVEREND. Were you there?

BILL. Sure!

PROFESSOR. You didn't answer when I signalled.

BILL. Sore throat.

SAM. So where's the swag?

BILL. The what?

SAM. The loot. The haul.

BILL. Oh, that. Right here. (HE *moves toward his gun pocket.* GANG *moves toward theirs*)

LILLIAN. (*Stepping in between* GANG *and* BILL) Leave Mr. Cracker alone! He's come a long way in the last few hours. On his spiritual journey, I mean.

BILL. Sure, kid, sure.

BABY FACE. That's real nice, Sister. But he ain't got too much further to go. So you better start thinking about a special prayer to say for him tonight, 'cause the next part of his trip is the hardest.

(SAM, *who has gone over to the window during this, lets out a shrill whistle*)

SAM. Cheese it, the cops!

(*Enter* COP)

COP. All right, you guys. Suppose you explain to me just what you was doing in the vicinity of the Manufacturers National Bank this evening? You first.

SAM. Me, officer? I took a drive out to Forest Park tonight. Yellow Cab. Ask the driver.

COP. And I suppose you got his number?

SAM. Sure, 352 —

COP. Skip it. You?

PROFESSOR. Hinky Dink Saloon, all evening, playing poker. Just ask Tessie Miller.

COP. Sure, sure. And you two?

BABY FACE. We was at a inanimate birthday party.

REVEREND. At Captain Wolf's.

BABY FACE, REVEREND & COP. Sixty East Oak Street.

COP. They sure do have a lot of birthdays there.

REVEREND. Large family.

BILL. (*Turns around*) Don't you have something to ask me, gumshoe?

COP. Bill Cracker! We've been looking for you. Question of the disappearance of a certain Dr. Nakamura.

LILLIAN. He's innocent, officer, completely innocent!

BILL. C'mon, what good does it do to lie now? (SHE *is*

stricken) I want to confess. I did it. I killed Dr. Nakamura.

(*The door flies open and* THE GOVERNOR *walks in.* EVERYONE
    gasps)

GOVERNOR. (*Sings*)
IF YOU WANT TO BE A BIG SHOT
START BY LEARNING TO BE TOUGH

BILL. (*Sings*)
CAUSE YOU'LL NEVER HIT THE JACKPOT
TILL YOU LIKE THE GOING ROUGH.

GOVERNOR.
ALL THE LITTLE SHOTS BELOW YOU
CAN BE BLOWN AWAY LIKE FLUFF

BILL.
IF THEY REALIZE WHEN THEY KNOW YOU
THAT YOU WON'T TAKE ALL THEIR GUFF

BILL & GOVERNOR.
JUST DON'T GET SOFT, BABY
FOR GOD'S SAKE NEVER GET SOFT, BABY
JUST KEEP ON POUNDING HIM RIGHT WHERE IT
    HURTS THE MOST
AND IF A LITTLE SHOT'S BIG NOISE SHOULD CAUSE
    A BOTHER
DON'T LET IT GET YOU DOWN, I MEAN YOU'RE
    NOT HIS FATHER.

JUST DON'T GET SOFT, BABY
FOR GOD'S SAKE NEVER GET SOFT, BABY
NO IFS OR BUTS
GO ON AND KICK HIM IN THE GUTS
GO ON AND KICK HIM IN THE GUTS

LILLIAN. Governor!
GOVERNOR. Miss Holiday, I am not dead! I had only a slight
wound, (*Takes off hat to show bandage on bald head*) and the
Canal outside is not so very deep. It was simple.
COP. All these crimes! But everybody is innocent!

(*Church bells begin to toll midnight*)

LILLIAN. I think this calls for a celebration! Merry Christmas everyone!

EVERYONE. (*Ad lib*) Merry Christmas!

(THE FLY *appears at the upstairs window, her gun drawn*)

FLY. Not that merry after all, my friends. Bill Cracker, your time is up.

(GANG, *including* GOVERNOR, *draw weapons and aim at* BILL)

LILLIAN. Stop! Don't let it happen now!

FLY. Too late, dearie. Two-timers don't get no second chance. Ready, boys?

HANNIBAL. (*Screams*) Sadie!

FLY. (*Seeing him, screams also*) Hannibal!

HANNIBAL. Darling!

FLY. My long lost husband!

(SHE *sings*)
WHEN OUR CHILDHOOD'S WARMTH WAS BANISHED
WE WERE WARMED IN LOVERS' ARMS
AND WE THOUGHT THAT WARMTH HAD VANISHED
LIKE OUR CHILDHOOD'S FADING CHARMS

HANNIBAL & FLY. (*Embracing*)
BUT THE SOUND OF CHURCH BELLS TOLLING
THROUGH OUR PAIN AND OUR DISMAY
SO INSPIRING, SO CONSOLING
IT HAS BROUGHT US HERE TODAY!

LILLIAN. (*Watching them embrace*) Well, Bill, I think it's time you and I got engaged.

BILL. Hold on! I have to think about that for a second.

FLY. (*To* HANNIBAL) And I have a small fortune to offer you.

HANNIBAL. (*Taking bank loot from her*) Why there must be over —

HANNIBAL & GANG. fifty thousand dollars!

HANNIBAL. in here. Where did you get it all?

FLY. Sewing, night after lonely night.

COP. (*Starting for sack*) Wait a minute . . .

HANNIBAL. I wouldn't know what to do with all this. (*Gives*

bag to MAJOR *just as* COP *reaches him*) Major, here, for the
good of the cause, in honor of my dear Sadie's return.

MAJOR. Accepted gladly, brother!

COP. (*Outmaneuvered*) Shucks!

LILLIAN. Time's up!

BILL. Awright, I accept.

(THEY *embrace. On a signal from* MAJOR, MARY *hurries into
kitchen and brings uniform back to* LILLIAN)

MAJOR. Sister Lillian! It's yours again. This is all your
work!

LILLIAN. My old uniform! (*As* SHE *puts it on*) Just think,
Bill, soon you'll be getting one, too! Our work starts tomorrow.

BILL. Well, I dunno . . .

(*Affectionate laughter.* GANG *has been conferring, and* REV-
EREND *now comes over to* LILLIAN)

REVEREND. Miss Holiday — I beg pardon for interrupting —
do you think we all might be able to join your little gang —
uh, group?

LILLIAN. What? You mean you all want to repent?

SAM. Well, you see, Miss, our line of work has suddenly
gotten every uninteresting.

PROFESSOR. We've decided we want to be more useful to
the world.

LILLIAN. That's the spirit! Major?

MAJOR. (*Who has been gazing into moneybag*) I'm astound-
ed! Mr. Wurlitzer, I'm now in a position to accept your organ.

SAM. (*Embracing her*) Field Marshal, you're a darling!

MAJOR. Why — I don't know what to say!

FLY. Then let me say it for you! Our two groups have been
fighting the same enemy all along. It's time to forget our little
quarrels and stand together. Blasting open a safe is nothing —
we've got to blast open the big gang that keeps the safe locked.
So slip on your brass knuckles and learn where to hit! Robbing
a bank's no crime compared to owning one! The world belongs
to all of us — let's march together and make it our own!

ALL. Hurray!

LILLIAN. (*Sings*)
LOOK ALL AROUND YOU

LOOK ALL AROUND YOU
LOOK ALL AROUND YOU, WE SEE YOU'RE ABOUT
    TO DROWN!
WE HEAR YOU SCREAMING "HELP ME!"
WE'LL CATCH YOU BEFORE YOU FALL DOWN
STOP ALL THE TRAFFIC NOW, LET'S CLEAR THE AIR
YOU WHO NEED HELP, KEEP YOUR HOPES UP,
    WE'RE HERE AND WE CARE
YOUR SOULS CAN STILL BE SAVED
BUT HEAR US, HEAR US, BROTHER, BEFORE YOU
    REACH THE GRAVE
THOUGH TROUBLES MAY BESET YOU
WE SWEAR WE WON'T FORGET YOU
THOUGH NOW YOU STAND IN NEED
THOUGH NOW YOU STAND IN NEED
DON'T TELL US, "THINGS WILL STAY THE WAY
    THEY ARE NOW."
THIS UNJUST WORLD WILL NEVER BE THE SAME

    EVERYONE.
IF ALL OF YOU WILL SWEAR TO STAND TOGETHER
FORGET YOUR FEARS AND MARCH WITH US TODAY
SO BRING ON THE TANKS AND THE CANNON
AND SQUADRONS OF PLANES LET THERE BE
AND BATTLESHIPS ON THE SEA

    LILLIAN.
JUST TO CONQUER ONE SMALL BOWL OF SOUP
    FOR EVERY POOR MAN
JUST TO CONQUER ONE SMALL BOWL OF SOUP
    FOR EVERY POOR MAN

    EVERYONE.
LET EVERY MAN COME JOIN US
OUR PURPOSE TO ENSURE
THE ARMY THAT IS GREAT AND STRONG
IS THE ARMY OF THE POOR

    LILLIAN.
FORWARD MARCH, CHIN UP, TAKE WEAPONS,
    PREPARE!
YOU WHO NEED HELP, KEEP YOUR HOPES US,
    WE'RE COMING, WE CARE!

(One last title on screen: THE happy *END)*

END OF PLAY

*(CURTAIN CALLS: EVERYONE sings the chorus of the "BIL-
BAO SONG." Second time through, either the lyrics are
projected on the screen, or BILL shouts them out for the
audience to sing along. During the calls SANTA CLAUS
appears at the upstairs window — drunk.)*

A NOTE ON THE ACTING

Happy End is a melodrama, not a burlesque of one, and should be played seriously, with acting that is crisp, not campy. Create your characters internally, like Method actors in a naturalistic play, then edit out as much of the surface as possible, heightening and giving a slight "edge" to the movements and gestures that remain. Delsarte's drawings are a good source of ideas, as are photographs of early 20th century theatre performances. At Yale Rep we tried something which became a tradition through several revivals: Early in rehearsal, we set parameters for the acting style by screening for the company a D. W. Griffith two-reeler starring Lillian Gish; and a German movie by Fritz Lang, who shared Brecht's interest in genre and worked with many of the same actors. For the Griffith film we always used *The Battle of Elderbush Gulch*, because it was in the Yale collection, but there are dozens of such films; the main points are the heightened style and the mystique of Lillian Gish, to whom Lillian Holiday owes so much of her persona. Any Lang film from the silent *Spies* onward will do, but the best choices in terms of acting are *M* and *The Testament of Dr. Mabuse;* the jeweler in the opening scene of the latter film is played by Theo Lingen, in a characterization similar to The Professor in *Happy End.* Notice how the German actors make very marked gestures and cut them short, as if they had a line around them; combine this with the high style of acting in the Griffith film. The same thing should be done with makeup — pick one feature and exaggerate it slightly. *Slightly.*

CHARACTERS

BILL CRACKER: An aging gangster-as-hero, late 30s, handsome in a battered way. He means business and looks it.

*LILLIAN HOLIDAY: Young, beautiful and intelligent. Tends to keep her emotions out of the way except when preaching.

THE FLY: A handsome woman of indeterminate age (not necessarily older). Tough and a good planner.

*DR. NAKAMURA ("THE GOVERNOR"): The Fly's second in command. A pickpocket by trade. Always polite and fastidious. Utterly ruthless.

*SAM "MAMMY" WURLITZER: A con man, voluble and sweaty; the gang's "front" man. Probably fat and seedy; there should be no indication of effeminacy. Bass.

JIMMY DEXTER ("THE REVEREND"): The gang's safe-cracker and explosives expert. Pompous, with a grave demeanor and a hollow, sepulchral voice — he used to be a tent-show preacher and a carnival pitchman. A thoroughgoing cynic.

BOB MARKER ("THE PROFESSOR"): The gang's mechanical expert, spluttery and excitable. Looks enough like the Reverend to have played his double in various con games. Can fix or repair any kind of gadget and is always fiddling with something. He always tries to get a word in and never can.

JOHNNY FLINT ("BABY FACE"): A large, young, ex-pug. Brain not inherently bad, but knocked silly from years of pummeling in the ring. Dumbly loyal, instinctively sees force as the answer to everything. Idolizes Bill.

MIRIAM: Common, but a beauty. Devoted to Bill who barely knows she exists.

*CAPTAIN HANNIBAL JACKSON: A few years older than The Fly. Not so much prissy as respectable. Has amnesia; prone to attacks of disorientation and migraine as the result of a blow on the head several years ago. Tenor.

SISTER MARY: A city girl. Raised decent and rather a snob about the fact. Late 20s, not beautiful. Dedicated in an officious way (think Prossy in *Candida*).

*SISTER JANE: A country girl, a few years younger than Mary. Pretty in a somewhat dumb way, sweetly pious, naive. Sweet soprano voice.

BROTHER BEN OWENS: Youngish. Just joined and anxious to make good. Takes an instant liking to Miriam.

MAJOR STONE: An imposing middle-aged woman. Comic only in that she takes herself and her job with such seriousness. Not a society dowager and not a cartoon bureaucrat.

THE COP: A Keystone cop. Use Mack Swain or Fatty Arbuckle as a model.

THE FOLD: They certainly are a scruffy lot — streetwalkers, vagrants, drunks, the respectable unemployed and homeless. They come mainly for the free soup and a few hours of warmth, but they do enjoy hearing Lillian preach a good rousing sermon — it's an age when public speaking is a form of entertainment. A smart director will a) encourage the building up of individual characterizations and b) be strict about cutting out any business that distracts from the main acion.

The Fold can be as small as six or as large as you like.

* indicates the characters who must sing well.

THE SET

The theatre at Yale had a permanent two-level stage which has had its effect on the planning of this script. In Act One and Act Three, Scene One, the upper level was the street and the bar was entered down a staircase stage right. For Act Two, the stairs were shifted to stage left, the pulpit replaced the bar, and the staircase now led to the upstairs rooms where the Army slept; Lillian's notes for the sermon and Bill's escape were played up there, also the Fly's surprise entrance in Act Three, Scene Two. The main entrance to the Army Mission was downstage left. This arrangment was followed again, with minor modifications, in the Broadway production. I'm not in love with it and have accordingly not included a ground plan of it in this script.

The basic requirements are very simple, as follows: The Beer Hall set requires two areas, the street and the saloon. The street must be large enough for The Fly's "faint" and the assembling of the Salvation Army to sing "Lieutenants of the Lord." The saloon needs a front entrance and a doorway (with a burlap curtain) to the back room. Bill's hatrack should be a prominent feature, and there must be at least one table with chairs. Also a nickelodeon or mechanical piano for the start of the "Bilbao Song."

The Salvation Army mission needs a raised dais for the Army to sit on during the service, a lectern or podium upstage center, and an area where The Fold's chairs can be set up. There are three entrances: A street door (not in the same place as the Beer Hall's), an exit to the kitchen and offices, and a separate area (it may be an upstairs) for Lillian's room. This last has the back window through which Bill escapes and The Fly enters. On or near the dais there is a small, shabby harmonium.

The main problem is the fast change required by the two "inset" bar scenes of Act Two. These must be fast, with an effect like silent-film cross-cutting. Attempting a full change from Army set to Beer Hall and back is not wise — too time-consuming. The most ingenious solution I've seen was in the second Yale production, where the Army froze in tableau, the lights changed to a single spot downstage left, and the Beer Hall was indicated by two stools and a Tiffany lamp that swung in from behind the proscenium arch on a hinged bracket. All you really need to do is be sure your inset area has enough space for the staging of the "Big Shot" number. The Army can even be visible during the Beer Hall insets, frozen and lit from behind or in dim sidelight. Use your imagination.

Be sure to remind your designers that this play takes place in Chicago in December. It's cold and windy, and there may be snow on the streets.

COSTUMES

BILL CRACKER: Natty 1910s gangster style, 3-piece suit and fedora. Elegant, not loud.

DR. NAKAMURA: Sleek black suit and wide-brim hat which he never takes off (till his "return" in Act Three). Ornate vest of some kind. Long Fu Manchu mustache. Carries cane with concealed sword in it.

REVEREND: Traveling preacher costume: Black coat and pants, checked vest, gold watch chain, possibly Amish hat, string tie.

PROFESSOR: Messy hair, gold-rim spectacles, plaid sport jacket and check trousers, papers in pockets — half burlesque-skit mad scientist and half racetrack tout.

BABY FACE: Big bulky-knit sweater, loud pants or plus fours, workingman's cap of some kind. His robbery costume is a Little Lord Fauntleroy outfit with short pants or golf knickers, a four-in-hand tie and a curly-locks wig.

MAMMY: Loud but coordinated checks or stripes, like a salesman at a convention. Flashy tie, rings, bright shoes. Maybe a straw boater, depending on how the weather is dealt with. His robbery costume is a respectable matron — dowager dress with beads, leg-of-mutton sleeves, fringed shawl, a turban or other kind of fancy ladies' hat and elaborate wig.

THE FLY: Late teens-early Twenties vamp costume, stylish, streamlined for efficiency — not overheavy on feathers or frou-frou, though she likes rich ornaments. Small expensive-looking jewels. Long cigarette holder. She must be able to change into it quickly from her newsboy costume, which is simply street-urchin coat, cap and baggy pants or overalls.

MIRIAM: Plain dress and apron. See photographs of Marilyn Miller in *Sally*. She might have *one* expensive bracelet.

THE SALVATION ARMY wears what it has always worn, except for Lillian who, after her dismissal, changes into a plain dark skirt, light blouse or shirtwaist, and shabby coat; little-girl straw hat with black ribbon. Battered suitcase.

WEAPONS

BILL: Gun in shoulder holster.

DR. NAKAMURA: Sword-cane. Long-barrel shotgun or small pearl-handled pistol in inside jacket pocket.

REVEREND: Bowie knife.

PROFESSOR: Small automatic — looks like it might be a cap pistol.

BABY FACE: One gun in shoulder holster or inside jacket pocket, another in outside jacket or pants pocket. Brass knuckles. Blackjack.

FLY: Lady's revolver in handbag.

FILM & SLIDES

The credit titles at the beginning, and the slide titles all the way through, are not essential and can be omitted if you don't have the budget or the projection facilities. They do, however, add a great deal in the way of atmosphere and charm. A good photographer with a sense of period style can make the pictures of the cast in costume look like real icons of the era, which adds to the strength of the production. If a slide is needed to fill time during any of the switches from the Beer Hall to the Mission in Act Two, the title "As the tension mounts . . . " may be added.

The robbery sequence in Act Three, Scene One has been done many ways: As a slide show, a silent film, a cartoon, a pantomime onstage and a shadow play. I prefer the film, which, again, helps define the genre of the work if done properly, but, again, there are many solutions available if you don't have the facilities for that one. (Bear in mind, too, that the shooting of the film, with the gang in costume and the location some actual bank in the area, can be wonderful publicity for the production.) The whole sequence can be omitted if you insist, but doing so is really a bad idea.

ASSIGNMENT OF SONGS

Because of differences between this adaptation and the original 1929 script of *Happy End*, certain songs or parts of songs are assigned differently in this text and the Universal Edition vocal score. Because the adaptor has survived several productions, there are also discrepancies in the English lyrics. This script is the final word on the subject and should be followed at all times.

One major variant should be noted: Brecht's lost lyric for the opening fox trot has been patchily reconstructed and is sung in German as part of the *Happy End* suite on Deutsche Grammophon's multi-disc Kurt Weill album (DGG 2563 585). A somewhat less musically dubious English version of this has been made by the adaptor and is recorded on Ben Bagley's *Kurt Weill Revisited*, volume 2 (Painted Smiles PS 1376). This material is not officially part of *Happy End* and may only be added with the express permission of the adaptor, who is reachable care of Samuel French.

THE PROFESSOR'S INVENTIONS

The lantern in the first scene is an ordinary outdoor lantern with one of its side panels removed and replaced by four metal reflector tabs. An ordinary floodlight bulb completes the effect of a primitive high-intensity beam. The handle might be removed to make it harder for the Reverend to hold.

The talking machine in Act Three is like an old-model two-way radio with a gramophone horn mounted on top, powered by a crank-driven generator at one side. Aside from the crank, it actually has only three working parts: Something to give off sparks when the crank is turned; a speaker hidden in the horn to broadcast The Fly's message; and the flash effect that goes off at the end. Beyond this, the designer and prop master can be as extravagant as they like; think Rube Goldberg. The Fly's mesage, by the way, should be spoken live on mike off-stage, and not pre-taped, for the sake of timing all the business and reactions.

If the Professor chooses, he can look smug instead of shocked when The Fly says, "I saw that." Everyone else double-take.

THE CHALK GARDEN

Drama. 3 acts. By Enid Bagnold. 2 men, 7 women. Interior.

An English gentlewoman lives with her granddaughter and devotes her life to simple if somewhat eccentric pursuits. Her chief concern is her garden, and her chief diversion is advertising for a companion to her granddaughter and then interviewing the applicants with full knowledge that she has no intention of ever hiring any of them. But one candidate is not so easily disposed of. She is an expert gardener, and such an excellent manager that the butler, who has always ruled the domicile, dies in a fit of exasperation. There is something strange about the woman, though, something in her past that must be discovered when a famous jurist comes to dinner. Despite all the sunlight and garden atmosphere, there is mystery here.
"Sparkling cut glass."—*N. Y. Times.* "A tantalizing, fascinating and stimulating piece of theatre."—*N. Y. Daily News.*

(Royalty, $50.00 where available.)

THE POTTING SHED

Melodrama. 3 acts. By Graham Greene. 6 men, 5 women. 3 interiors.

A suspense story of high intellectual calibre, this begins with the return of an unwanted son at the time his father is on his death-bed. His mother will not permit him to see his father in his last moments, and he is estranged from every member of the family. Why? What had he ever done? The key apparently is in an event that happened in the potting shed when he was 14 years old. The son's mind is a blank on the subject; his mother is silent; his psychiatrist meets a stone wall. Beginning with the widow of the old gardener, proceeding to the church where his uncle is pastor, and ending in a family Christmas reunion, the son pieces together the total intelligence about that dark event in the potting shed.
"A detective story for grown-ups. Brilliantly wrought entertainment. . . . It has bite, it has drive, it has wit."—*N. Y. World-Telegram & Sun.* "An intellectual detective story . . . profoundly interesting."—*N. Y. Daily News.*

(Royalty, $50.00 where available.)

Musical Productions Controlled by

Samuel French, Inc.

PLAIN AND FANCY
SEVENTEEN
THE MERRY WIDOW
WONDERFUL WALTZ
THE VAGABOND KING
THE DESERT SONG
OF THEE I SING
GOOD NEWS
THREE TO ONE
THREE WISHES FOR JAMIE
THE GINGHAM GIRL
THE FIREMAN'S FLAME
OH! SUSANNA
NAUGHTY NAUGHT
THE GIRL FROM WYOMING
MY CHINA DOLL
ROSALIE RUNS RIOT
THE SWEETEST GIRL IN TOWN
LITTLE WOMEN
OUR NIGHT OUT
HARMONY HALL
THE BACHELOR BELLES
THE PRINCESS RUNS AWAY
GOLDEN DAYS
THE TALES OF HOFFMAN
OLD KING COLE

A descriptive list of "French's Musical Library"
will be sent on request.

NO, NO, A MILLION TIMES NO!

A musical mellerdrammer. Book, Eskel Crawford. Lyrics and music, Bud Tomkins. 4 males, 8 females. Chorus of males and females. One easy set. Old-fashioned costumes. Time: 1 hour.

Something that is absolutely original. A one-act old-time melodrama with music. The plot has to do with Stafford Blackman, the villain, luring Nellie Quackenbush, the innocent farmer's daughter, to the big city for the purpose of wedlock (so she THINKS!) but when Nellie gets there, she senses he "won't do right by Nell," so she flees while she is still "pure as the driven snow," and returns to the farm and the arms of her country sweetheart, Noble Hart. Each book contains the full text with stage directions and piano score.

Amateurs may produce this musical comedy free of royalty, upon purchase of at least 12 copies. $5.00 royalty for each additional performance. No orchestrations.

PISTOL PACKIN' SAL

A hillbilly musical comedy. Book, Eskel Crawford. Lyrics and music, Bud Tomkins. 7 male, 7 female (extras if desired). One easy interior. Modern and western costumes. Time: 1 hour.

Sal, daughter of Sheriff Skinner, has been appointed his "deppity" during his absence. Into the lunch room that Sal runs comes a good-looking young stranger who has been in an auto accident, and who becomes the chief suspect in a holdup. Sal has "fallen" for him on sight, but the shadow of suspicion threatens her new happiness. The stranger, too, has "fallen" for Sal. Together they manage a happy conclusion. Each book contains the full text with stage directions and the piano score.

Amateurs may produce this musical comedy free of royalty, for one performance, upon purchase of at least 14 copies. $5.00 royalty for each additional performance. No orchestrations.

Witness for the Prosecution

Melodrama—3 Acts

By AGATHA CHRISTIE

17 Men, 5 Women. Interior—Modern Costumes

Winner of New York Critics Circle Award and the Antoinette Perry Award. One of the greatest mystery melodramas in years.

The story is that of a likable young drifter who is suspected of bashing in the head of a middle-aged, wealthy spinster who has willed her tidy estate to him. His only alibi is the word of his wife, a queer customer, indeed, who, in the dock, repudiates the alibi and charges him with the murder. Then a mystery woman appears with damaging letters against the wife and the young man is freed. We learn, however, that the mystery woman is actually the wife, who has perjured herself because she felt direct testimony for her husband woud not have freed him. But when the young man turns his back on his wife for another woman, we realize he really was the murderer. Then Miss Christie gives us a triple-flip ending that leaves the audience gasping, while serving up justice to the young man.

(ROYALTY, $50-$25.)

The Mousetrap

The longest-run straight play in London history.

Melodrama—3 Acts

By AGATHA CHRISTIE

5 Men, 3 Women—Interior

The author of Ten Little Indians and Witness for the Prosecution comes forth with another English hit.

About a group of strangers stranded in a boarding house during a snow storm, one of whom is a murderer. The suspects include the newly married couple who run the house, a spinster, an architect, a retired Army major, a strange little man who claims his car overturned in a drift, and a feminine jurist. Into their midst comes a policeman, traveling on skiis. He no sooner arrives than the jurist is killed. To get to the rationale of the murderer's pattern, the policeman probes the background of everyone present, and rattles a lot of skeletons. Another famous Agatha Christie switch finish! Chalk up another superb intrigue for the foremost mystery writer of her half century. Posters and publicity.

(ROYALTY, $50-$25.)

&&&&&&&&&&&&&&&&&&&&&&&&&

THE SENTIMENTAL SCARECROW

(ALL GROUPS)

MUSICAL-COMEDY-FANTASY—1 ACT
Book and Lyrics by S. Charles Shertzer
and Music by Nathan Brown

A musical version of Rachel Field's "The Sentimental Scarecrow." 2 men, 5 females, and a band of gypsies. (Exterior) Modern Costumes. 5 songs, incidental music, and a gypsy dance.

The Scarecrow is exactly what the title suggests; he wishes to become a human; in order to realize his wish, he must convince some young lady to not only kiss him, but to agree to marry him. The fun of this production is found in the Scarecrow's antics as he attempts to win a wife. The music and the lyrics are delightfully amusing, plus exciting, and at times filled with genuine pathos.

The songs include "Half the Day's Gone," "A Cold Stare and a Withering Glance," "Gypsy Caravan," "I've Got to Have a Dame," and "Funny Looking."

Music on rental and deposit, write for information.

Royalty, $15-$10.

A Pink Party Dress

MUSICAL—1 ACT
David Rogers and Mark Bucci

A musical version of Margaret Bland's "Pink and Patches." 1 man, 3 females. (Exterior) Modern Costumes. 5 songs. 35 minutes.

The story of Texie, a mountain girl who hopes to escape the life of hardship and poverty her mother and other mountain women lead. She longs for the richer life she has observed at a fashionable hotel nearby and for a pink party dress instead of the patched brown denim she is forced to wear. Then a visitor to the hotel offers to give Texie a dress. Whether her proud mother will allow her to accept it and whether it will be the Pink Party Dress form the story of this charming folk musical.

The songs include "Women Folk Work Fer Men Folk," "A Pink Party Dress," "Lovely Evening, Isn't It?," and others. Complete libretto and piano score.

Royalty, $15.00 first performance
$10.00 each additional performance.